PORTSMOUTH
SHIPS, DOCKYARD
& TOWN

PORTSMOUTH
SHIPS, DOCKYARD & TOWN

Ray Riley

TEMPUS

Portsmouth Point, formerly known as 'Spice Island', showing in the foreground the Round Tower, dating from 1418-20, but rebuilt by Henry VIII. In the middle ground is the Camber, with the Bridge Tavern on the right and the Isle of Wight ferry terminal to the left. Behind the car ferry is the Gunwharf Quays development, within which is the Vulcan storehouse. (*Institute of Maritime and Heritage Studies, University of Portsmouth*)

First published 2002
Copyright © Ray Riley, 2002

Tempus Publishing Limited
The Mill, Brimscombe Port,
Stroud, Gloucestershire, GL5 2QG
www.tempus-publishing.com

ISBN 0 7524 2776 8

TYPESETTING AND ORIGINATION BY
Tempus Publishing Limited
PRINTED IN GREAT BRITAIN BY
Midway Colour Print, Wiltshire

Contents

Acknowledgements

I would like to record my gratitude to the many people who have contributed to my understanding of Portsmouth's history, but particularly to the late Robert Sutherland Horne who nearly four decades ago triggered my interest in the dockyard; to Deane Clark for his invaluable architectural comments; to Brian Patterson and Archie Malley of the Portsmouth Royal Dockyard Historical Trust for their substantial help and advice in the selection of photographs from their archive; and to Louis Shurmer-Smith, Director of the Institute of Maritime and Heritage Studies at the University of Portsmouth for his permission to use a number of outstanding aerial photographs of the Portsmouth scene.

Note on the text

For the sake of simplicity, photographs appearing by permission of the Portsmouth Royal Dockyard Historical Trust are acknowledged by the letters PRDHT after the caption.

Introduction

No two towns are alike, however much they may superficially appear to be, but even on first acquaintance some are very different. The contrast between Portsmouth, a naval dockyard town, and the not too distant ancient cities of Winchester and Chichester is striking. The differences do not end there, for although it was for long a major shipbuilding and repairing town, Portsmouth was unlike the great commercial shipyard towns of Newcastle and Glasgow, where fortunes were made by the building companies and by sub-contractors and suppliers, and where as a result a substantial middle class arose, contrasting with the situation in Portsmouth. Because Portsmouth Dockyard was a government establishment, profit did not exist, and because there was a high degree of self-sufficiency within the dockyard, there was limited opportunity for local suppliers. One industry that did develop, not with the dockyard as its market, was the manufacture of clothing, particularly corsets, based on the availability of female labour for which there was no call in the dockyard. In fact until the inter-war period, in terms of the number of industrial jobs, clothing was approximately equal in importance to shipbuilding. The outcome was that until the 1970s and 1980s, when long-term contraction was effected in the dockyard, Portsmouth was a town with a naval dockyard and clothing manufacture at its core, with a number of activities such as brewing and public utilities supporting its largely artisan population.

Since the 1970s Portsmouth has undergone substantial change as the significance of both the dockyard and the clothing industry has dwindled, there has been an influx of activities such as mechanical and electrical engineering, while the office and service sector has become increasingly important – the university is now the single largest employer in the city. The oldest part of the dockyard has been converted to a Heritage Area including the historic ships *Mary Rose*, *Victory* and *Warrior*, while some of the surrounding forts have become museums. In place of bucket and spade holidays on Southsea beach, we now have 'heritage tourism', with the dockyard at its centre. And just as the dockyard was established because of its proximity to France, nearness to the old enemy has been used as the basis of a continental ferry port which is now the second largest British passenger port. Where once the harbour was replete with the passage of naval vessels, it has now become host to large car ferries plying to Cherbourg, Caen, Le Havre and Bilbao in Spain.

Partly because one way to explain the present is to delve into the past, and partly because the past is interesting in its own right, the emphasis of this book is historical. The first chapter follows change until 1840, something of a watershed in naval architecture since it was in the 1840s that steam propulsion became important in warships. The second chapter concentrates on the dockyard and warships prior to the First World War; it is a fortunate fact that although the ships are no more, the buildings and docks used in their construction, fitting out and repair remain intact, forming the basis of the heritage tourism industry. Chapter three is concerned with the industries, including transport, of the town before 1914; very little remains of most of these activities, but fortunately photographs taken at the end of their lives provide an important record of what was. The final chapter looks at events in the twentieth century, but without attempting detailed comment on the new factories on suburban industrial estates and on recent office developments. The photographs bring together a number of impressions of warships and dockyard scenes by John Green, with more formal shots of naval craft, the harbour ferries, the Isle of Wight catamarans and car ferries, and the continental car ferries. Portsmouth's maritime endeavours are as strong as ever.

The oldest member of the Brittany Ferries fleet, *Quiberon*, heading for the continental ferry port, with T42-type destroyer, *Edinburgh*, tied up at South Railway Jetty in the dockyard.

One

Portsmouth and the Sail Navy before 1840

For long Portsmouth has been known as a Dockyard town, and indeed until the 1980s, when the last great contraction of the yard took place, this was certainly the case. Portsmouth's original function was not so much that of a dockyard, since these did not exist, so much as a landing place for the convenience of dignitaries travelling between France and England, following the Norman conquest. A wall was constructed in 1212 at the landing place, near the entrance to HMS *Vernon*, now Gunwharf Quays, but this was short-lived, and it was not until the end of the fifteenth century that the monarch – Henry VII – saw fit to invest in Portsmouth once more. A dry dock for repair work, the first in a royal dockyard, was completed in 1496, and on site were a storehouse, forge and smithy. The 80-ton *Sweepstake* was launched in 1497, so it is likely that a building slip also existed at this time. Portsmouth's most famous ship, the 500-ton *Mary Rose*, was completed in 1509, although repairing was more important than building. *Mary Rose* foundered near Southsea Castle in 1545 as she manoeuvred to engage the French off the Isle of Wight, but after years of painstaking recovery of artefacts, what remained of the hull was raised from the seabed on 11 October 1982 and carefully preserved in the dockyard. In the later years of Henry VIII's reign – he died in 1547 – and throughout that of Elizabeth I, the yards on the Thames were developed at the expense of Portsmouth, and in 1623 the dry dock was filled in, causing Sir George Blundell to remark in 1627 that the town was 'a poor beggarly place, where is neither money, lodging nor meat'. Indeed, being a naval dockyard town, Portsmouth's fortunes were closely linked to war and peace, rather than to the market considerations which governed most towns' growth.

The Commonwealth era from 1649 saw Portsmouth's star in the ascendant once more, as a building programme was inaugurated to clear the Channel of pirates and royalist ships. The appropriately named 422-ton *Portsmouth* was launched in 1650, the first ship to be built in the yard for more than a century. A double dock was authorised in 1656, and by 1660 seven warships had been completed; between this date and the end of the Third Dutch War in 1674 no less than eighteen vessels were launched. The dockyard was now firmly established, a fact confirmed by the construction in 1663 of an enormous wooden ropehouse some 1,000ft long.

Between 1658 and 1677 the yard trebled in area. Meanwhile the size of vessels was also increasing: *Royal Charles*, completed in 1673 was 1,443 tons. Yet for the workforce, the end of hostilities brought redundancy for many, only 220 being retained. However, Portsmouth was favoured by the arrival of the Protestant William of Orange on the throne in 1688, for the new monarch was opposed to Catholic France, and the town's location was well suited to actions against the enemy.

In 1692 under the supervision of Edmund Dummer, Surveyor to the Navy Board, a plan for the remodelling of the dockyard was initiated. An enclosed Great Basin was built, allowing the repair and fitting out of ships without interference from tidal variations. Giving in to the Basin was the Great Stone Dock; it was the first dock in the country to be constructed of stone rather than wood. It also had stepped sides to facilitate the insertion of wooden beams to shore-up vessels. The graceful curves at the head of the dock, reflecting the bow section of contemporary ships, are still to be seen. Inevitably modifications have been carried out in its 300-year life, but it is still the oldest artefact in Portsmouth Dockyard. At the same time to the north Dummer built a second but much larger basin, access to which was through a small, conventional wooden-sided dock, on the site of the present No.6 Dock. The logic of this arrangement is unclear, for the sheer size of the basin suggests that frequent access to the sea would be required, rendering the use of the wooden dock for repairs questionable. South Dock, which no longer exists, was completed in 1703. The larger basin survives beneath the Block Mills (see below). To support these developments, the workforce rose from 294 in 1687 to 1,271 in 1697. By 1711 more than 2,000 people were employed, making the yard possibly one of the largest

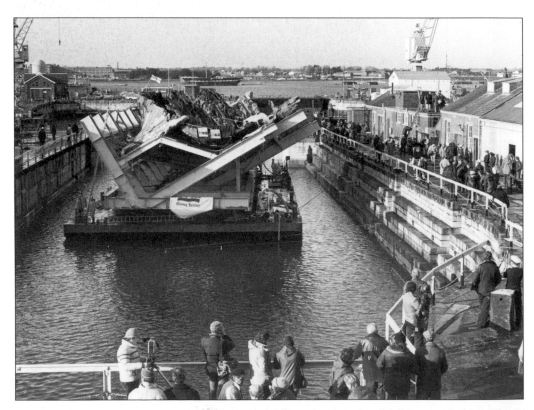

The hulk of *Mary Rose* floating into No.4 dock aboard a specially constructed cradle in 1982. She was launched at Portsmouth in 1509. In the harbour is *Foudroyant*, for many years a training ship. *(PRDHT)*

The last docking of the training vessel *Foudroyant* in 1905. She was launched as the frigate *Trincomalee* in Bombay in 1817, became a drill ship in 1861, and in 1897 a training ship, when she changed her name. She left Portmouth for Hartlepool in 1991.

manufacturing enterprises in the country. It is easy to overlook the problems there must have been in co-ordinating the efforts of such a workforce, when much information was passed by word of mouth, and thus easily misinterpreted. It was not until more than 150 years later that enterprises of such size emerged in the commercial sector.

Shipbuilding was spurred on by the Seven Years War, 1756-63, some fourteen ships being launched in the 1750s and 1760s. *Britannia*, completed in 1762, was 2,116 tons. The American War of Independence, 1775-83, saw the numbers employed rise to 2,471. Despite the upturn in output, there were inefficiencies in the dockyard which were unearthed during a Navy Board visitation; the outcome was the plan of 1760. A building slip which had been constructed to issue into the Great Basin, full of ships under repair, was removed and relocated so that it gave directly into the harbour. In its place a second stone dock was completed in 1772 (now No.4 Dock). Following a series of fires, it was accepted that although they were more expensive to construct, brick buildings were a sounder long-term investment than those made of wood. In heritage terms this was an important decision, for almost all the buildings in the Dockyard Heritage Area, now recognised as probably the finest remaining set of eighteenth-century industrial structures in Britain, date from this period. On the left-hand-side, proceeding from the dockyard gate to the *Victory*, are three similar storehouses. They are timber framed and, at ground floor level, they have arches which until the 1980s were closed by large wooden doors. The northernmost store was completed in 1763, the storehouse centrally located, boasting an impressive clock tower which rang out dockyard time, was finished in 1776, while the southernmost was completed in 1782. The storehouses were able to receive supplies by means of Camber quay, constructed between 1773 and 1785. Similar buildings were to be found in commercial ports, but their size usually caused them to be replaced, making the Portsmouth group an unusual survivor. On the other side of the road, opposite the central storehouse is the 1,095ft-long ropehouse of 1776, in which ropes were made on the ground floor and hemp spun on the floors above. The roof was once punctuated by dormer windows, removed in the early 1950s. At the far end is the Hatchelling House where fibres were carded ready for spinning. Parallel with the ropehouse are three hemp stores, finished between 1771 and 1782. To the east of *Victory* were four buildings erected between 1786 and 1790 which doubled as stores and workshops, with an open court at their centre; three remain, as does South Office Block, just ahead of *Victory*, dating from 1786. This gives a total of twelve structures, all but two of which can be viewed from the Heritage Area.

Hard on the heels of the American War came hostilities with the French. It became apparent that there was still insufficient repair and fitting-out capacity to deal with the many ships built by private builders at Cowes, Bursledon and Beaulieu. During the 1770s alone fifteen vessels built at Beaulieu were fitted out in the yard, and between 1773 and 1814 some forty-six commercially-built vessels were fitted out at Portsmouth. To effect the necessary changes, in 1796 Samuel Bentham was appointed Inspector General of Naval Works. He more than doubled the size of Dummer's Great Basin, enclosing it with a pontoon, or caisson (pronounced casoon in Portsmouth) to allow the passage of horse-drawn carts, impossible with V-shaped gates, and thus saving many a trip round the land side of the Basin. Two docks leading from the Basin were added: No.2, which now holds *Victory*, and No.3, now host to *Mary Rose*. A third, No.1 Dock, was completed just to the south of the Basin with direct access to the sea, the monitor M33 now occupying this dock. Bentham's docks differed from Dummer's in two important respects. Their entrances were designed as an inverted arch, thus tying together each side and ensuring that the gates and caissons fitted snugly, reducing water leakage. Secondly, their bottoms had a slight slope, causing water to drain to their entrances, which were at different levels, water moving by gravity to the deepest, from which it was pumped into a sump.

A view of the ninety-eight-gun *Boyne*, converted to other duties, moored off the Gunwharf ordnance depot in 1826. (*Drawn by Henry Moses*)

All Bentham's structures, completed in 1803, remain in place, with little modification even after two centuries of use. With these new facilities it is not surprising that in 1810, for instance, some eighteen times more man-hours were expended on repair than on shipbuilding. By 1814 the yard was employing 3,878 men.

Not only was Bentham an engineer, but he was also acutely cost conscious. One of his justifications for the extension of the Great Basin was that it would reduce the payment of 'afloat-time', for which shipwrights travelling to and from ships moored at sea were eligible. He persuaded the Navy Board that it made economic sense to make a small payment to dockyardmen, termed 'chip money', in place of their right to remove from the yard pieces of wood less than 3ft in length. The 'dockies' had been sawing spars in lengths of 2ft $11\frac{1}{2}$in and using the wood for chairs, table legs, cupboards and the like, giving rise to a peculiar domestic vernacular architecture in Portsea. Unfortunately no evidence seems to have survived. Bentham used his powers of persuasion to get the Navy Board to pay for the sophisticated pulley block-making machinery, designed by Marc Brunel, which could drastically reduce production costs. Indeed, the savings made possible were such that the costs of the machines were met within four years, and their life extended to more than a century and a half. There were forty-five machines in total, the last being installed in 1806; they were the world's first example of metal machine tools used for mass production. By ensuring that the output of one machine was related to the capacity of the next machine in the production process, Bentham and Brunel can lay claim to be pioneers of production engineering in addition to their other attributes. Some of these machines are on view in the Dockyard Apprentice Museum in the dockyard, although their historical significance is not made clear.

Brunel's machines had to be housed; Bentham's space-saving solution was to build the Block Mills over Dummer's larger basin which was used only as a reservoir, at the same time installing a steam engine – the first in a naval dockyard – to drive the machinery by day and to pump out the docks by night. Aware of the risk of fire, Bentham built a water tank into the roof of the Block Mills. As a fire precaution he also constructed a huge elevated tank containing 740 tons of water, linked to buildings in the yard. The supporting structure for the tank was rebuilt in iron in the 1840s, and is one of the few examples of Bentham's work that cannot be seen by a discerning visitor to the Dockyard Heritage Area. Bentham's contribution to Portsmouth Dockyard was substantial, but possibly because he was a contemporary of Nelson, his achievements remain almost totally unsung. He did not suffer fools gladly, continually seeking to change the established order of things, and he was effectively dismissed from his post in 1805 when he was dispatched to Russia on a mission which was bound to fail. He was apparently offered £6,000 not to return!

It is sometimes said that the pulley block mills with their use of steam power and production line machinery signalled the beginning of Portsmouth's industrial revolution. Yet the high degree of organisation overall and the separation of work into a large number of specialised tasks, characteristic of the dockyard for more than a century, suggests that the Industrial Revolution took place in the naval dockyards well before the age of steam and iron. These advances notwithstanding, the end of the war against France in 1815 resulted in the inevitable contraction of the workforce, which fell to 2,079 by 1830. However, the 1830s witnessed yet another resurgence of the dockyard, not so much for political as technological reasons. The Admiralty ordered the construction of steamships, thus ensuring that employment was maintained, and in fact showed a slight increase to 2,227 in 1841. The new vessels had paddle wheels, their engines and boilers being fitted into wooden hulls, but the yard was incapable of fitting them out, and they had to be engined elsewhere. Thus the 712-ton *Hermes*, launched in 1835, was engined by Maudslay & Field on the Thames. It was to be more than ten years before Portsmouth was in a position to play a fuller role in marine engineering.

In order to reduce costs and at the same time to ensure quality, the Navy Board followed a policy of self-sufficiency, so that materials such as timber and hemp for rope were bought in, but processing was undertaken inside the yard. There were therefore saw pits, a ropehouse, sail-making facilities, a rolling mill producing copper sheaths for ships' hulls, and an iron foundry. Even the milling of flour for bread and biscuits for ships' crews was carried out at King's Mill, which used to stand approximately at the entrance to what is now Gunwharf Quays, and which worked by the force of tidal water escaping from the millpond. The pond is now the naval recreation ground. Additionally the brewing of beer, the baking of bread and the salting of meat were undertaken in Old Portsmouth in establishments run by the Victualling Board. The consequence was that there was almost no opportunity for local contracts, and Portsmouth's manufacturing base remained firmly in the hands of the government. The principle was continued in the late 1820s when it was decided that the victualling facilities in Portsmouth were inadequate, and that operations should be transferred to what became in 1831 the Royal Clarence Victualling Yard in Gosport. At the centre of the new structures was a four-storey grain store mounted on cast-iron columns, its front flush with the water's edge to facilitate the unloading of grain directly from vessels below. The notion of a warehouse with a working quay beneath, rather than between it and the sea, or dock, had been used by Telford at St Katharine's Dock in London in 1828. With the demolition of Telford's building, the Clarence Yard granary becomes the oldest structure of this kind in the country. To the north of the granary a substantial bakery was built. It incorporated nine ovens capable of baking a ton of bread, or 10,000 'hard tack' biscuits an hour. Dough was prepared by a series of machines designed by Thomas Tessel Grant, the Yard Storekeeper (commander). Both the granary and the bakery may easily be seen from the Portsmouth-side of the harbour (especially with binoculars), but the corn mill, which had ten pairs of stones powered by a 40hp steam engine, is located behind the granary and not therefore visible from Portsmouth.

As will be apparent from the work of Dummer, Bentham and Brunel, the dockyard at Portsmouth was host to a number of developments of an internationally important scale. Inevitably the yard provided the town's core employment, and indeed in 1841 one-third of Portsmouth's industrial workers found work there. However, that the percentage was not more is initially surprising; what is even more surprising is the importance of the clothing industry which, together with tailoring and shoemaking, accounted for almost one half of the town's industrial workers in 1841. Quite apart from the needs of the local population, there was considerable demand from sailors since until free uniforms, which were not even recommended until 1858, the practice was for the ship's purser to buy garments ashore and then sell them on to the crew. It is conceivable that this doubled the market for Portsmouth's clothing makers. A further reason for the relative importance of clothing was the dockyard's self-sufficiency, which reduced the number of ropemakers, sailmakers, nailmakers and iron founders working outside the yard. These trades flourished in commercial shipbuilding centres.

Bread being the staple diet caused baking to be an essential part of the industrial scene, as was flour milling, which in Portsmouth, lacking water power (King's Mill apart), was the province of windmills. There were eight such mills in 1830. Because windmills are such a distinctive feature of the landscape, they appear on maps of the period. There were two groups: five on the western shoreline between Rudmore and the dockyard, and three on Southsea Common, exposed to the westerly winds. By far the largest was New Dock Mill, located in what is now Napier Road, constructed in 1817 by a group of dockyardmen forming the Dock Mill Society, whose earlier mill dating from 1799 and near the dockyard, had been commandeered by the Board of Ordnance for extensions to the yard. This was an early example of self-help among working people; flour was produced for sale to members at well below the market price. New Dock Mill was the only windmill to survive the nineteenth century. There are no remains of the mills themselves, but Dock Mill Cottages adjacent to New Dock Mill have been refurbished and are in occupation.

Not surprisingly in a naval dockyard town and a garrison to boot, brewing was a vital ingredient, with two particularly large breweries in Penny Street, Old Portsmouth, owned by the Carter and Garrett families, and another sizeable affair in St George's Square, Portsea,

An 1825 harbour scene, ranging from warships, including *Bulwark* on the left, the hulk *Boyne* adjacent to the Gunwharf ordnance depot on the right, to harbour wherries. Even the wooden mooring posts bears a government arrow. *(Drawn by Henry Moses)*

also belonging to the Carters. Brewing was unusual among Portsmouth's industries in that it was the only one which generated long-term profit in the best capitalist tradition, and whose leading members achieved real social standing. When Daniel Garrett died in 1808, his brewery was inherited by his sons, one a Vice Admiral and another the captain of the Portsmouth garrison and a knight of the realm. Sir John Carter was succeeded in 1808 by his son who was MP for the Borough for twenty-two years from 1816. However, the physical evidence of these breweries has disappeared, making the survival of the eighteenth-century dockyard buildings all the more remarkable. Similarly nothing remains of the first two gasworks in the town. One was constructed in 1821 in North Street, close to what is now Unicorn Gate in the dockyard. Rising demand occasioned a relocation in 1834 to Flathouse where coal could be directly unloaded from colliers. Production continued at this site until the mid-1960s.

Insignificant in terms of numbers employed, the short-lived Portsea Canal, which ran between Milton and Landport from 1822 to 1831 – the present day Allders is on the site of the basin – is nevertheless an interesting episode in transport history. It was killed off by litigation from people whose wells had been salinated along its route, and by the use of Portcreek to gain access to Portsmouth Harbour from Langstone Harbour. Despite nearly two centuries of disuse, the brick sea lock at Milton is in reasonable condition, having been renovated by the City Council, while the tall engine house, which pumped sea water into the canal, may be seen in nearby Waterlock Gardens. It is still possible to walk along the towpath as far as Milton Road, after which the canal disappears beneath Goldsmith Avenue. Preserved in its original condition is the small Southsea lighthouse, built by the Admiralty in 1823 actually on Southsea Castle. It lies at the head of the deepwater approach to the harbour, and to simplify navigation ships would line up the lighthouse with the spire of St Jude's Church when the latter was completed in 1852.

Victory in Portsmouth Harbour in 1828. The small vessel alongside is a collier. *(Drawing by Edmund Cooke)*

Southsea Castle, 1543-44. Built on the orders of Henry VIII to protect the deepwater channel against the threat of a French attack. It represents a transition stage between curved and straight lined walled fortifications. *(Institute of Maritime and Heritage Studies, University of Portsmouth)*

The main gate of the dockyard, 1704. The photograph was taken before the bicycle revolutionised the dockyardmen's means of transport. The gate was widened in the Second World War to allow the passage of fold-wing aircraft used on aircraft carriers. *(PRDHT)*

Landport Gate, 1760, St George's Road. This is the only one of the six Portsmouth and Portsea town gates to survive in its original position. This is a view from within the town of Portsmouth, the outer entrance being on the right beneath the cupola. Until around 1873 this was the main entrance to the town.

Above: The Hatchelling House, 1771, where hemp was carded prior to being spun for rope making, is on the left, and the Ropery, 1776, on the right. The arched structure between the two was used as a walkway between the two buildings. It was unusually strong and in 1813 the right-hand arch was blanked off, becoming the fixed point for chain testing apparatus.

Left: Lion Gate, 1777, which stood at the eastern end of Queen Street, Portsea. It was preserved when the fortifications were demolished and in 1929 built into the Dockyard Semaphore Tower, which had been destroyed by fire in 1913. *(PRDHT)*

Opposite top: Unicorn Gate, 1778. One of the Portsea town gates, formerly at the north end of North Street, rebuilt into the wall of the Dockyard Extension in the early 1870s. *(PRDHT)*

Fort Monckton, 1790-95, Stokes Bay. This was the only fort of those round Portsmouth built to engage both seaward and landward approaches. The west-facing ramparts on the left are still clearly visible. (*Institute of Maritime and Heritage Studies, University of Portsmouth*)

Above: A drawing of vessels in the Great Basin *c*.1795, before Bentham's extension work. South Office Block lies in the centre, behind which is the ropehouse, and to the right Nos 9, 10 and 11 storehouses.

Left: A sheer hulk, that is, a vessel fitted with tall sheer legs, used to fit out ships moored in the harbour or Spithead. They were the predecessors of floating cranes.

Opposite below: The austere, Georgian lines of South Office Block, 1787-89. The central section with three arches was added in 1840, and the porches probably at the same time.

Although modified, some of the original features of the Great Stone Dock of 1698 survive, notably the chutes on the right-hand-side and the elegant stonework at the head of the dock.

Stonework laid down at the main (now Victory) gate in the dockyard to represent the trackways used before the arrival of the railway. Such smooth stone slabs facilitated movement of vehicles over what was otherwise uneven cobbles.

The stern of *Victory*, emphasising the graceful and intricate woodwork then built into warships at the time.

The 1,095ft-long ropehouse, 1776, a truly enormous building by the standards of the day.

No.10 Store, 1776, photographed in 1973, since when the doors have been removed to make a walkway to the *Victory*. The clock tower, which used to signal dockyard time, was destroyed in the Second World War.

From the left, Nos 9, 10 and 11 Stores, 1782, 1776 and 1763 respectively. The clock tower above No.10 Store was replaced in 1991. Photographed in 1992.

East Hemp House, 1781. Buttresses have been added for strength; the date of the building is worked into the brickwork in the gable end. *(PRDHT)*

No.6 Dock, originally built of wood in 1698, but much modified in the eighteenth century. It is the smallest dock in the yard.

Victory as she was in 2002.

The Block Mills, 1801. Their importance lies in what took place within, rather than in their architecture. The wall centre left is the remaining section of Dummer's Great Basin of 1698.

The interior of the Block Mill taken from a postcard sent in 1905.

A view of the overhead line shafting in the Block Mills. The beams and circular columns are of wood, adding a distinctive aura to this important early factory. Photographed in 1968.

The swing-arm circular saw designed by Marc Brunel to cut the lignum vitae, used for the pulley block wheels, was built into both the floor and the ceiling of the Block Mills, and for this reason it remains in situ. Photographed in 1968.

Marc Brunel's scoring engine in the Block Mills in 1968. It was later transferred to No.6 Boathouse.

Marc Brunel's mortising engine from the Block Mills on display in the Dockyard Apprentice Museum in No.7 Boathouse.

Marc Brunel's shaping engine used in the Block Mills, now in the Dockyard Apprentice Museum. As the main frame rotated, the wooden blocks within it also rotated; thus at each main frame rotation a different part of the pulley block was cut.

Above: The caisson at the entrance to the Great Basin, 1801. Bentham's caisson was made of wood and was replaced by an iron structure in the 1840s.

Right: The Dockyard Semaphore Tower, *c.*1810. The Sail Loft is to the right and the Rigging House to the left, both built in 1784. In the foreground is the railway viaduct constructed in 1876 linking South Railway Jetty to Portsmouth Harbour station. The Semaphore Tower was burnt out in 1913. *(PRDHT)*

The Vulcan Storehouse, 1815, at Gunwharf ordnance depot. It suffered bomb damage in the Second World War, but much remains within the Gunwharf Quays development of 2000. (*PRDHT*)

The Camber, Old Portsmouth. Excavations in the foreground reveal the footings of the swing bridge at this site until 1923, hence the name Bridge Tavern. The photograph, taken in 1971, also shows the inter-war coalbunkers behind the pub, and on the right the extensive transit sheds. The Camber was Portsmouth's historic port.

The Camber, Old Portsmouth. Repair work in 1971 indicates the small scale of operations: the narrow quay and the small vessel tied up. In the background are the cranes of the Camber Dock.

The Camber, Old Portsmouth. A roller fairlead and a cannon pressed into service as a bollard give the impression of a small port, which is what the Camber has always been. Photographed in 1972.

Portsea Canal pumphouse, Milton, 1822. The tall beam engine house, which pumped seawater into the canal, stands out from the surrounding houses. It has been in residential use since the 1830s.

Portsea Canal, Milton sea lock, 1822. The seaward end gates have gone and the brickwork is deteriorating, not surprisingly since the canal ceased operations in 1830. Since this photograph was taken, in 1968, the City Council has refurbished the lock.

Above: The derelict lock gates at the western end of the sea lock of the Portsea Canal at Milton, photographed in the 1930s. There was a second lock chamber beyond the infill, near the houses in the distance.

Right: Southsea Castle lighthouse, 1823. Since the stretch of water between the Castle and the Isle of Wight was only four miles, there was no need for the usual tall edifice, but the lighthouse did mark the deepwater approach to Portsmouth Harbour.

The granary, mounted on iron columns, and to the right the bakery, at Royal Clarence Yard, Gosport, opened in 1832.

Detail of the iron columns and beams supporting the granary at Royal Clarence Yard. The design was by John Rennie.

Two

The Dockyard and Ships 1840-1913

Experiments in steam propulsion began in the dockyard in 1821, but its general introduction into naval vessels was a slow process owing to the restriction of fire power caused by the space taken up by paddle wheels, and the vulnerability of paddle wheels to enemy guns. It was not until 1845, following the epic tug-of-war between the paddler *Alecto* and the screw-driven *Rattler*, both with similar engines, ending with a decisive win for *Rattler*, that steam propulsion could justifiably be used in warships. The first screw-driven vessel to be built at Portsmouth was the 483-ton *Rifleman*, launched in 1846, but engined on the Thames by Miller & Rosenhill. Two years later the very much larger *Arrogant*, 1,872 tons, was completed; in the same year the last sail warship, the 1,987-ton *Leander*, entered the water. The advent of steam power called for a range of trades new to the dockyard, as engineers, fitters, boiler-makers and foundrymen were recruited, often from the private sector throughout the country, to deal with the new technology. By 1851 there were almost 3,000 workers employed in the dockyard.

Having made the decision to embrace steam technology, the Admiralty was obliged to undertake a major reorganisation of the Portsmouth yard. This was entrusted to Royal Engineer officers, comprising Lt-Col. Henry Brandreth, who was Director of Admiralty Works at Greenwich, and at Portsmouth Capt. Roger Beatson, whose plan was finished in 1843, and then later Capt. Sir William Denison and Capt. Henry James. The central feature was the construction of a seven-acre Steam Basin (Bentham's basin was a mere two acres), together with two docks, Nos 7 and 8, which were longer and narrower than their predecessors, allowing them to accommodate the new ships coming into service. This additional length notwithstanding, it was later thought advisable to build in 1858 a further dock, No.10, backing on to No.7, enabling the two to become a single, very long dock if need should be. This proved a prescient strategy, for until 1863 it was the only way the new breed of ships such as *Warrior* could be dry docked. Oddly enough, to No.7 and 10 Docks belongs the doubtful honour of being the first docks to be filled in since the eighteenth century; they are now car parking space. The Steam Basin, which was largely built by convict labour in the charge of the contractor, Benjamin Bramble, a local man, was opened by the Queen on 25 May 1848.

The propeller from the *Rattler* which in 1845 defeated the paddler *Alecto*, thus demonstrating the efficiency of the screw propeller. The propeller is on the ground floor of No.10 Store on the walkway to the *Victory*.

The most visible piece of architecture in the new scheme was the Steam Factory, which runs along the western side of the Basin. Some 600ft long, it is an elegant structure in rich red brick and Portland stone, designed by Denison. Its narrowness was determined by the need to avoid internal columns which would have interfered with the movement of heavy equipment by the gantry crane. Adjacent, a large Smithery was completed in 1852. It was originally designed to match the Steam Factory, but as an economy measure the frame was clad with corrugated iron. The interior iron columns are similar to those used in the Great Exhibition hall, cast by Fox Henderson. To the west of the Smithery, in 1847 two building slips were given iron roofs (to protect the ships, not the shipwrights), the span of each being 90ft, greater than that of the railway train sheds of the day. The ironwork was by Baker & Son, Lambeth, but the design work was almost certainly by one of the Royal Engineer officers, probably Capt. Denison. The roofs were demolished in 1980, the argument being that there was an earlier structure preserved at Chatham Dockyard. To the south of the Steam Basin a large Iron Foundry, designed by Capt. James but architecturally similar to the Steam Factory, was opened in 1854, completing this industrial complex based on steam and iron. It was served by a railway line opened in 1849 extending from the main line station, passing over Commercial Road by means of a level crossing, and breaching the Portsea fortifications at their northern end, close to the harbour shore. At the same time Capt. James provided wagons with wheels capable of working on both the granite tramway, introduced to facilitate the movement of wheeled vehicles, and on the standard gauge system. The tramway was lost under later road surfacing, but in 1999 a short length was laid down close to the Victory Gate, unfortunately without signage.

Separate from the group of new buildings and the Steam Basin, two buildings were constructed at the same time in the older part of the dockyard. Facing the Mast Pond, which is near the main gate, a boathouse to the design of Capt. Beatson was constructed in 1846 for the building and repair of small craft used to take shipwrights and sailors to and from vessels moored in the harbour and Spithead. In constructional terms this boathouse is probably the most important in the yard, for behind the bland exterior its internal cast iron beams are supported by underslung wrought iron trusses, a novel method of adding strength to the structure. This impressive ironwork can be seen by visiting the current Action Stations centre now on the ground floor. Not too distant from the boathouse, but outside the Heritage Area, is the Chain Test House, where the strength of chains was ascertained. It has a granite and iron ballast floor to prevent erosion from chains being dragged along; the roof is carried on columns and beams similar to those supporting the Bentham's Water Tank, rebuilt in iron in 1846.

The outbreak of the Crimean War in 1853 provided an impetus for ship construction, and more importantly, so did the perceived threat of war with France. Between 1853 and 1862 some twelve warships were launched, seven of which being larger than anything previously constructed. They belong to what is an interesting transition phase in naval ships, for although they possessed steam engines and screw propellers, they also carried sails and were wooden hulled, even though iron ships had been built for some years; Brunel's *Great Britain*, launched in 1843, is a fine example. The upsurge of activity in the yard was reflected in the numbers employed, which reached 4,633 in 1860, but at the same time there were important changes outside it. It had become apparent that new artillery technology was such that the dockyard could be attacked from vessels in the Spithead, rendering the Portsmoth and Portsea fortifications irrelevant. These were therefore demolished in the 1870s and in their place were constructed four sea forts and twelve land forts, to the west of Gosport and along the line of Portsdown Hill to guard against a landward attack. The forts were dubbed 'Palmerston's Follies', since in the event the French never invaded.

While warships were wooden hulled, increases in size were possible only in small increments. But once iron, and later steel, was employed, substantial additions to size became possible, aided by improvements in the efficiency of steam engines. This latter was an important point since the early engines were so inefficient that much valuable space had to be devoted to coal

No.6 Boathouse, 1846, flanked by No.7 Boathouse on the left, and No.5 Boathouse on the right. Boats gained access to the mast pond in front of No.6 Boathouse through lock gates beneath the road, and were hauled up the ramp and into the Boathouse. The plain exterior belies the sophistication of the interior ironwork.

bunkers. The consequence of the changes was that in the 1850s both the French and the British built larger steam warships with armour-plated hulls, yet which retained sails for use when conditions were favourable. The French *La Gloire* and the British *Warrior*, launched on the Thames in 1860, were the lead vessels of this type. Recognising that even bigger ships than the 9,137-ton *Warrior* were feasible, the Admiralty delegated the task of designing further extensions to the Royal Engineers. Col. Sir Andrew Clarke's plan for what came to be known as 'The Great Extension' was ready in 1864, only sixteen years after the opening of the Steam Basin. The area of the dockyard was almost trebled, from 99 to 261 acres, half the area being reclaimed from the harbour and much of the remainder deriving from land released by the demolition of the Portsea fortifications. Three enormous basins, each larger than the Steam Basin, were constructed for fitting out, rigging and repairing, while three docks were also provided. The work, which began in 1867, was completed in 1881, long after the threat of a French attack had passed. Dredging, the removal of spoil, and the transport of stone blocks were carried out by steam-operated equipment laid on wooden piling driven into the mud. The spoil was dumped on Whale Island which eventually became large enough to be used as a naval gunnery training establishment, HMS *Excellent*. Much of the labour was provided by convicts, who also made bricks on site from clay found on site. Despite subsequent changes within the dockyard, the outer limits of the yard have remained virtually unaltered since the completion of the Great Extension.

Inevitably such a dramatic increase in capacity resulted in the construction of new production facilities which related to the needs of metal ships and new types of armament. The first of these was the Armour Plate Workshop of 1867, whose Italianate twin entrances represented the last of the truly architecturally distinctive buildings in the yard. The Gun Mounting Shop was opened in 1886, incorporating six bays each with a travelling crane for moving the very heavy guns of the period. Opened in the same year was the Torpedo Store, itself indicative of the new weapons being deployed by the fleet. A torpedo testing range was completed in 1889 by the amalgamation of Great and Little Horsea Islands in the north of the harbour; this now forms part of Port Solent Marina. Gas supplies for lighting were drawn from the nearby Flathouse gasworks, and were metered in the remarkable surrounds of a mock

The mast pond in front of No.6 Boathouse crammed with small craft in 1901.

The interior of No.6 Boathouse showing the underslung trusses supporting the main beams. Each beam was cast with an identifying letter to simplify construction. Photographed in 1984. *(PRDHT)*

seventeenth-century stone tower complete with ports for riflemen, completed in 1886. To facilitate the transfer of materials in the yard, the standard gauge railway was gradually extended to serve the new docks and basins; at its peak the system had twenty-five miles of track. The extension of the main line railway to the harbour station in 1876, made possible by the removal of the fortifications, provided an opportunity for the Admiralty to require the railway to build a single line branch to South Railway Jetty in the dockyard. A small waiting room with characteristic valancing has survived; the ornate train shed for the convenience of visiting dignitaries did not appear until 1893. At the same time a track was laid into the ammunition depot, Gunwharf, lying on the south side of the Harbour station. The original line into the dockyard was retained, but the track was re-laid to link with the High Level station at Portsmouth Town, thus removing the need for the Commercial Road level crossing. By 1881 there were 6,300 workers in the dockyard; many of the artisan houses put up at this time may still be seen in Buckland, Copnor and the eastern part of Southsea.

Not strictly part of the dockyard, but an integral part of naval operations, was Gunboat Yard at Gosport, developed during the 1850s. In 1859 it was said to have had the capacity to repair 120 gunboats simultaneously. The ships were hauled out of Haslar Lake up a ramp and moved into the covered working area by means of a traverser powered by a steam engine. It is sometimes possible to visit Gunboat Yard during the annual Heritage Days.

The ships launched in this era, following the disappearance of French enmity and prior to the rearmament race with Germany, nevertheless gradually grew in size and sophistication as new technologies became available. The early history of *Royal Sovereign* reflects the speed of change. She was designed as a traditional vessel, but altered to screw propulsion while on the building slip, launched in 1857, and completed in 1862 at 3,765 tons. However, demonstrating the new armament technology, her upper decks were later removed to allow the installation of five 10½in muzzle-loading guns, each weighing twelve and a half tons mounted in turrets firing 300lb shells. She was the first British capital ship to have her main armaments outside her hull. Her 2,460hp Maudslay engines gave her a speed of 11 knots and her sails were restricted to three auxiliary jibs. The invention of an effective condenser in the early 1860s allowed the employment of high pressure steam in compound engines which, in relation to the power they delivered, occupied a modest amount of space, as did the coal required to fuel them. There was thus no need to economise through the use of sail. How different from *Frederick William*, a first rate ship launched only a few years before in 1860 with 110 guns in traditional fashion.

In the sense that she had no sails at all, *Devastation*, 9,380 tons, launched in 1871, was the pioneer of the new age. Additionally her armament was substantial, for she had four 12in, 35-ton rifled (giving much greater range and accuracy than was possible than with smooth-bore artillery) muzzle loaders firing 714lb shells, mounted in armour-plated turrets powered by steam. Moreover, her top speed was 13 knots. She was described at the time as 'an impregnable piece of Vauban fortification with bastions mounted upon a floating coal mine'. Of even more massive proportions and fire power was *Inflexible*, 11,800 tons, launched in 1876. She had four 16in 80-ton rifled muzzle-loading guns, mounted in 750-ton twin turrets. She was the first warship to have submerged torpedo tubes, her side armour was 2ft thick, and she was provided with electric light and anti-roll tanks. It seemed as though each vessel completed incorporated a new innovation. *Colussus*, 9,150 tons, launched in 1882, counted five 6in breech-loading guns – much more efficient in operation than muzzle loaders – as part of her armament. The armoured cruiser *Imperieuse*, 8,500 tons, launched in 1883, was equipped with a variety of guns, including four 9.2in, ten 6in and four 6lb guns, rather than a small number of very large guns which typified *Inflexible*. *Camperdown*, a battleship of 10,600 tons launched in 1885, positively

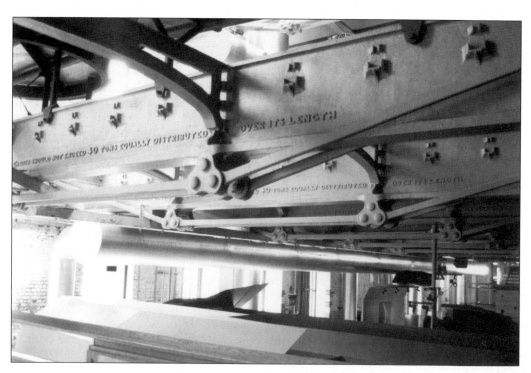

Detail of a main beam with its underslung truss in No.6 Boathouse, 1846. Photographed in 2002.

bristled with twenty-two big guns and five torpedo tubes as well. The battleship *Trafalgar*, completed in 1887 was, at 12,590 tons, the largest ever built at Portsmouth; her eight torpedo tubes represented increasing faith in this form of weaponry. It has to be said that not all innovations had a positive outcome, for there were occasional disasters which brought hard times to many a Portsmouth family. No better example exists than that of *Captain*, an experimental turret ship with a very low freeboard, but an unduly high centre of gravity, commissioned in Portsmouth in 1870. She capsized in the Bay of Biscay on her first voyage with the loss of 472 lives, mostly Portmuthians. In one Portsea street alone thirty wives were widowed. A public fund in aid of the dependants – there was no provision for widows at the time – raised £57,824, but could only have been a small compensation.

Despite the construction of these large warships, and of others of a smaller size, the fact remained that Portsmouth continued to be primarily a fitting out and repairing yard. In order to fulfil this role, and because it was becoming apparent that an arms race with Germany was under way, two further docks were built in 1889 and 1897 on the south side of the repairing basin. Two additional locks, C and D, were built to improve access and completed in 1914, the walls separating the three original basins were removed to create a single, vast No.3 Basin. The northernmost No.5 building slip was also doubled in length. The factory, said to be the largest covered space in the world at the time, was opened in 1905. Apart from its size, its appearance is unremarkable, representing the new architectural industrial style of the twentieth century. Apart from the demolition of the 250-ton cantilever crane, such a prominent feature of the Portsmouth skyline between 1912 and 1984, the removal of No.5 Slip in 1980 and the installation of more modern cranes, this whole complex remains largely as it was, more than a century ago. It may be visited when the dockyard is open to all on Navy Days or the Festival of the Sea.

As the turn of the century neared, warships became truly enormous. *Royal Sovereign*, a battleship of 14,150 tons, launched in 1891, carried four 12in and ten 6in guns, and was protected by waterline armour 11in thick. She was not made of wrought iron, but of steel, a material which offered the same strength but yet was lighter than iron, so giving economies in fuel consumption. From *Royal Sovereign* evolved the *Majestic* class of 15,000 tons displacement. *Majestic* herself was launched in 1895, followed by *Prince George*, also in 1895, *Caesar* in 1896, *Canopus* in 1897, *Formidable* in 1898 and *London* in 1899. *London* was modified in 1912 to permit the launch of an aircraft from her fore gun turret. Substantial though this building programme might have been, it was Admiral Fisher's *Dreadnought* project, agreed in 1905, which brought Portsmouth to its apogee. The yard was selected to build the 17,900-ton *Dreadnought* itself, armed with ten 12in guns in five twin turrets and no less than twenty-seven 12lbers, and launched in 1906 after only 130 days, sailing for trials a year and a day after being laid down. In place of triple expansion engines, *Dreadnought* was fitted with steam turbines which had been demonstrated so effectively by Charles Parsons in *Turbinia* at the 1897 fleet review. The prototypes of the subsequent *Dreadnought* classes were all built at Portsmouth: *Bellerophon*, *Neptune*, *Orion*, *King George V*, *Iron Duke* and *Queen Elizabeth*, 27,500 tons, launched in 1914. *Queen Elizabeth* was the first warship to be equipped with 15in breech-loading guns; she was also oil-fired, on many grounds a much more effective fuel than coal. Slightly less than one-quarter of *Dreadnought* tonnage was built at Portsmouth, rather more than on the Clyde, arguably then the greatest commercial shipbuilding area in the world. Yet after 1915 no further capital ships left the Portsmouth slips. In 1911 over 10,000 workers were employed in the yard. For all the innovations in the ships themselves, shipbuilding was still a labour-intensive process. Ships' plates were positioned largely by human effort, the riveting of plates was achieved by two men with hammers (some 655 riveters and drillers were on the strength in 1914) and slipway cranes were simple derricks. On the other hand the census returns reflect the advent of yet another innovation wave, for while there still 341 shipwrights working with wood on small boats, and some 2,764 working with metal, there were 929 electrical engineers, dealing with radio, lighting and searchlight equipment.

Above: The Steam Factory, or No.2 Ship Shop, 1848. Some 600ft in length and architecturally the most elegant industrial building in the yard.

Left: Detail of the Steam Factory, 1848. Beneath the pediment is a round-headed window which could be opened to admit materials hoisted by a wall crane, the base of which remains. The lavish use of Portland stone adds to the general impression of distinction.

Opposite below: This caisson has had its water pumped out and is floating, affording a view of its shape, deck and 'bow' which fits into the dock entrance wall.

The original entrance to the Steam Basin, 1848, was closed by a metal caisson which was uncovered during road resurfacing in 1984. It was boat-shaped fore and aft and had cantilevered bars to take the decking at each end. When a bigger entrance was constructed at another point, the original caisson was simply sunk in situ.

Above: The launch of *Dauntless* in 1847. It was fitted with a 520hp steam engine and weighed 1,575 tons. Behind are the seldom illustrated covered building slips.

Left: The roof and ironwork of No.3 building slip, 1847. The slip was eventually filled in and a track for an overhead gantry crane added when it became a shipbuilding shop. It was demolished in 1980. Photographed in 1968.

Opposite below: Chain Test House, late 1840s. Each chain had to pass a test of its strength. After the 1860s this was achieved by means of hydraulic power. Discernible is the floor made of metal castings bearing a government arrow and 'Po' for Portsmouth. *(PRDHT)*

Fire Station, c.1846. The original structure designed by Bentham consisted of wooden supports for a tank from which water could be moved to other buildings in the event of fire. It was replaced with the present iron structure in the 1840s and came to be used as the dockyard fire station.

The Iron and Brass Foundry, 1848, probably by Capt. W. Dennison. It became the Small Brass Foundry once the much larger Foundry was completed in 1854. Photographed in 1984.

The entrance to No.8 Dock, 1850, illustrating the inverted arch principle developed by Bentham.

The Smithery, 1852. By comparison with other contemporary buildings the Smithery was mundane, although it did herald the large-scale use of corrugated iron.

The large steam hammer in the process of forging metal in the Smithery, 1901. Note the two swan neck cranes on either side of the hammer to position the metal being forged.

The interior of the Smithery, photographed in 1968. The heavy equipment matches the bulk of the anchor.

The Iron Foundry, 1854. The architectural similarity with the Steam Factory is obvious even behind the unfortunate clutter. As a fire precaution a water tank was built on the roof and an interior sprinkler system provided.

Right: As part of the attempt to minimise fire risk in the Foundry in 1854, staircases were made of metal and flooring was carried on brick arching laid on iron beams. Fire doors were also installed. Photographed in 1984.

Below: The launch of *Victoria* in 1859, to be fitted with a steam engine; she weighed 4,127 tons. The delicate ironwork of the roof trusses is faithfully recorded, which is more than can be said for the scale of the people present.

Warrior, 1860, at her berth outside the dockyard. Were it not for the funnels, she might be mistaken for a sailing ship.

Fort Brockhurst, 1858-63, Brockhurst. Built on the assumption that invading forces would make a landward attack from the west. It was one of a chain of five forts on the western side of the harbour. Noticeably, there was a reversion to the medieval practice of a keep within the outer walls. (*Institute of Maritime and Heritage Studies, University of Portsmouth*)

Horse Sand Fort, 1880. One of the four sea forts guarding the approaches to Portsmouth. Built of granite with iron reinforcement, it had ports for forty-nine guns together with moveable turrets on the roof. (*Institute of Maritime and Heritage Studies, University of Portsmouth*)

The Great Extension 1867-76. The major problem at the outset was the softness of the mud, which meant that dredging had to be effected on piles. The photograph shows a steam-powered bucket dredger at work in 1868.

The Great Extension. Rather than have railway track conflicting with work on the floor of the docks and basins, a high level track was constructed. Here four-wheeled wagons and a locomotive may be seen delivering masonry, which was lifted into position by a travelling steam crane or crab. Photographed in 1868.

The Great Extension. A view of the travelling steam cranes, or crabs, on their overhead trackway. Using one steam engine they could not only lift material, but also propel themselves from side to side and along the dock. Photographed in 1870.

The Great Extension. In this photograph, taken in 1870, may be seen the railway for the delivery of stone blocks and an interesting section through the dock bottom and wall.

The entrance to the Armour Plate Workshop, 1867. This was one of the last decorative structures built in the dockyard. The headings to the windows and the entrance are of rich, red rubbed brick, contrasting vividly with the more subdued brickwork elsewhere. Photographed in 1984.

The turret ship *Captain*, which capsized on her maiden voyage in the Bay of Biscay in 1870.

Gunboat Yard, Gosport, drawn in 1872. Under cover are a number of *Blazer* class gunboats. Outside is the steam-powered traverser which moved the boats to and from the ramp rising from the sea. *(PRDHT)*

The tender *Horning* being winched up the ramp from Haslar Lake at Gunboat Yard, Gosport. The traverser is just visible to the left. *(PRDHT)*

No.7 Boathouse, 1875, built on metal piles above the mast pond. It was wooden clad and was given tiny eighteenth-century windowpanes.

To facilitate bending of wood a steam kiln was used. This one is in No.7 Boathouse, 1875, now housing a café and the Dockyard Apprentice Museum. Despite its late date, the boathouse columns and beams are wooden. *(PRDHT)*

The fine low relief above the entrance to the Torpedo Store, 1886.

The RN Torpedo School, located aboard *Vernon*.

The remarkably ornate dockyard gas meter house, 1886. Some of the casemates of Frederick's Battery, 1688, relocated from the harbour in 1870, are visible on the left.

No.13 dock, completed in 1876 and extended in 1905 to handle the warships of the *Dreadnought* class. The crane supports on the left-hand-side were a later addition.

Coaling Point, 1876. The striking-looking cranes are hydraulically operated.

Right: The frigate *Calliope*, 2,770 tons, launched at Portsmouth in 1885. She became a drill ship in 1907.

Below: Victory in the harbour when she was used as a training ship.

The Mould Loft, 1891, where full-sized templates of ships' plates were laid out on the floor. Photographed in 1984.

No.2 slip was unusual among dockyard slips being equipped with rails on which a cradle bearing ships could move. The toothed rail in the centre was a braking system for the cradle. The whole was known as a 'patent slip'. Photographed in 1979.

The steam winch, by Cowans Sheldon, Carlisle, 1896, for No.2 patent slip. Photographed in 1979.

Horsea Island patent slip, 1894. One method of getting a boat out of the water was to construct a dry dock. Another was to employ a cradle mounted on a ramp. This one on Horsea Island, which was used for torpedo testing, was probably employed to winch up boats carrying these weapons. The Roman Portchester Castle is in the background. Photographed in 1971.

The remains of the dockyard's biggest building slip, No.5, extended at the end of the century, with the Steam Factory in the background. Photographed in 1979.

South Railway Jetty train shed, 1893. Sometimes referred to as the Royal Shelter. One of the most ornate railway structures ever built, it was for the convenience of dignitaries who frequently travelled in naval vessels when on official visits. The rail link to the main line was removed in the 1950s, but the shed remains, beautifully maintained.

The Painters' Shop, 1896, borrowing from the style of buildings half a century older. Photographed in 1992.

Canopus, launched in 1900, being fitted out at Portsmouth. Photographed in 1901.

Left: About to leave to join the Mediterranean fleet from Portsmouth is the battleship *Implacable* in 1901, launched at Devonport in 1899.

Below: Royal Sovereign, the largest warship to have been launched at Portsmouth, in 1892.

Above: An unfortunate incident. En route to the breaker's yard in Hamburg on 23 October 1903, *Neptune* collides with *Victory*. She was not in steam and was in the charge of two tugs.

Right: A battleship under construction before the First World War. The absence of cranes was a notable feature of shipbuilding at this time. (*Drawing by John Green, 2001*)

The scale of The Factory, 1905, is obvious from this photograph. There were in fact five bays under the same roof. Photographed in 1980.

Coming alongside South Railway Jetty – the train shed is just discernible centre right – on 8 May 1906 is *Renown*, with the Prince and Princess of Wales on board. *(PRDHT)*

Launch of the battleship *Bellerophon* on 27 July 1907. Before being fitted out ships had a somewhat forlorn appearance, contrasting with the powerful-looking paddle tug, and indeed the steam pinnace. *(PRDHT)*

The launch of the *Iron Duke* at Portsmouth on 12 October 1912. *(PRDHT)*

The battleship *St Vincent*, launched at Portsmouth in 1908. She had a rather short life, being sold under the Washington agreement in 1921. *(PRDHT)*

Right: An old cruiser and four dockyardmen. *(Drawn by John Green)*

Below: Submarine B11, launched in 1906, coming into Portsmouth Harbour, with another submarine and Camper Nicholson's boatyard in the distance. She sank a Turkish frigate in the Dardanelles in 1914, the exploit securing her entire crew a medal. *(PRDHT)*

To facilitate the movement of the largest vessels in and out of No.3 Basin, two new locks, C and D, were constructed just prior to the First World War. The photograph, taken in 1910, illustrates some interesting cranes, especially those on the raised level to the right; they appear to be self-propelling.

Princess Royal entering C Lock at its opening on 8 April 1913.

The construction of a new dock under way. Photographed in 1911.

In an attempt to provide additional, relatively cheap dry dock facilities, a floating dock was commissioned. Arriving in 1912, it was located immediately outside the north-east corner of the yard. The crane-like structure on the right is one of two arms which were joined during sea travel; a man is standing on the top of the left-hand arm. The battleship *Monarch* was launched at Barrow in 1911. *(PRDHT)*

Above: The huge 250-ton electric cantilever crane erected in 1912, designed by Sir William Arrol & Co. It was the prototype for several others in dockyards round the world. *(PRDHT)*

Left: The burnt-out shell of the Semaphore Tower, 1913.

North Pumping Station, 1913. A little-known decorative structure housing the pumps for the last extensions to the yard. The use of electric machinery accounts for the small size of the pumphouse.

Monitor M33, 1915, lying in Bentham's No.1 dock. It is being conserved by Hamphire County Council.

Three

The Industries of the Town 1840-1913

In complete contrast to the efforts of the dockyard, which round the turn of the century was one of the world's largest shipbuilding centres, Portsmouth's commercial shipbuilding sector was tiny, and comparable to that in many small ports round the country. One possible reason for this stunted development was the control of the shoreline by the Admiralty, which was reluctant to sanction activities which might interfere with the movement of naval ships. Moreover, the Board of Ordnance was not prepared to allow the fortifications to be breached by a railway line, making it difficult for the port at Old Portsmouth, known as the Camber, to grow. By the time the fortifications were razed in the 1870s, the railway companies did not consider it worthwhile to run a line to the Camber. In each of the decades between 1840 and 1879 slightly more than 2,000 tons of shipping were launched, the average vessel size varying between fourty-four tons and seventy-nine tons. The largest ship built was the 386-ton *Dahlia*, constructed by J.T. Crampton in their Mile End yard in 1878. The firm of John Read had a patent slip in Old Portsmouth reputed to be capable of accommodating an 800-ton vessel, but since the largest craft built by Read and subsequently registered in Portsmouth displaced only 180 tons, it is reasonable to suppose that the firm was more involved in repair than construction work. Support for this is provided by the Borough Council's decision to finance a dry dock in the Camber for repair work, on the assumption that the existence of the facility would attract traffic to the port. The dock was opened in 1863, but since 1982 has lain beneath the Isle of Wight ferry car park.

Despite the example set by the dockyard, outside it there was reluctance to invest in steam power. Not until 1872 was a steam vessel launched, and then only the 9hp *Queen*. The following year the 70-ton *Southsea*, operated by the Southsea & Isle of Wight Steam Ferry Co. was launched, Crampton built three small steamboats between 1875 and 1883, and the 60-ton *Lady Busk* was produced by H. Tipping in Old Portsmouth in 1881. The last two decades saw a marked decline in activity, which largely involved hoppers and barges: Crampton and Frank Bevis, also at Mile End, built little else between 1890 and 1910. Out of this sorry state of affairs rose one firm which not only endured, but also made its reputation through the production of naval vessels. Herbert Vosper set up a small engineering works on Old Portsmouth in 1869 and diversified into boat and engine building six years later. Five of his boats were registered in Portsmouth between 1894 and 1906; one was the 11-ton *Aorangi*, powered by an 8hp oil engine, which thus avoided the need for a boiler and space for coal. An indication of the respect his boats commanded was the use of one by Edward VII for a fleet review, in spite of the production of small craft by the dockyard. This was followed by an order from the Admiralty, and the purchase of Read's yard in the Camber.

As a consequence of the dockyard's policy of self-sufficiency, the domination of the market for marine engines by national builders on the Thames, Tyne and Clyde, and the weakly-developed and backward commercial shipbuilding industry in Portsmouth, there were scant opportunities for an engineering industry. Naturally some firms in this sector did emerge, such as McKinley at Mile End and J.W. Tout in Landport, but they were general engineers employing a dozen or so workmen on small orders, repair work, and the installation of equipment in small factories in the town. On the other hand, there was much more scope for the metalworking industry, for its market was closely related to housebuilding – kitchen ranges, footscrapers, manhole covers and locks – and to roads which required lamp posts and grid covers. Street furniture by George Cash, W.H. Sperring, John Shervell and H. Evans still abound in Portsmouth, even if their foundries are no more. Curiously enough one small works, Treadgold in Portsea, which originated in the 1780s, has survived, largely because in addition to jobbing foundry work, it possessed a hardware shop selling all manner of nuts, bolts, screws, nails, hinges and the like. After the business closed down in 1988 the property was bought by Hampshire County Council and converted to an unusual museum, in which everything, including the dust, has been left as it was. We are afforded a fascinating glimpse of what such premises were like in the nineteenth century. In the office there are even stand-up desks, one of which is equipped with a speaking tube.

W.H. Sperring, Albion Iron Works, Clarendon Street, Landport, established in 1854. Although apparently derelict, the foundry was still working, even though its days were numbered, the site having been acquired by the Council for housing. The removal of old houses between the foundry and Fratton Road affords a view of the Florist pub in the distance. Photographed in 1972.

W.H. Sperring, Albion Iron Works. Workmen charging the reheat furnace with coke and scrap to make molten iron for moulds. Metal escaping from the leak at the bottom of the furnace was collected and used. Photographed in 1972.

Commercial shipbuilding and engineering might have been unimportant, but oddly enough for a port, the clothing industry was particularly well developed. In 1841, the first year for which detailed occupation data are available in the census, no fewer than 45% of Portsmouth's industrial workers were employed in this sector, that is far more than the numbers in the dockyard. During the remainder of the century the imbalance evened out; by 1871 the dockyard was in the lead and the share of clothing had fallen to 38%, where it remained for the next forty years, in spite of the expansion of the dockyard. In 1911, there were more than 10,000 working in the manufacture of clothing, yet contemporary accounts of the town suggested that everything revolved round the building of *Dreadnoughts*, indeed, most people today are surprised by the statistic. Comparison between the proportion of clothing workers in Portsmouth with the proportion in the country as a whole, shows that in 1851 the share of clothing workers in the workforce was twice that in England and Wales. Towards the end of the century, Portsmouth's specialisation declined, but one branch stands out: the manufacture of corsets. In 1851 there were proportionately fifteen times as many corset-makers in Portsmouth as the proportion in England and Wales, and in 1871 there were still twelve times as many. This represents the kind of specialisation we associate with Kidderminster (carpets), Luton (hats) and Honiton (lace), but because of the importance of the dockyard, is not generally known, even in Portsmouth.

The reason for the importance of the clothing industry lies in the characteristics of a naval dockyard town, which influenced wages in a number of different ways. Firstly there was almost no call for female employment in the dockyard, and few opportunities, other than domestic service, outside it. Secondly, the fluctuations in the numbers needed in the dockyard encouraged women to bolster family income. Thirdly, for much of the century ships' crews were paid at the end of a commission, and wives probably received nothing while their men were absent. Fourthly, the soldiers of the garrison could also be sent on an overseas posting, and their families would suffer in the same way. As a result there was a surfeit of women seeking work, which ensured that wages were low, and at the same time women were suited to the making of clothes. In these circumstances entrepreneurs were encouraged to set up a warehouse, or use a house as one, from which women would collect material to work on at home. The logical next step was for the organisation of production on a factory basis, but only in the corset branch did this occur. In fact, corset-making and brewing were the only two private sector industries which were characterised by a good number of factories. The first corset factories, as opposed to warehouses, date from the 1850s. By 1905 there were seventeen, employing 3,000 people in 1911, almost all of them in Landport, which as a result could lay claim to be the town's industrial area. The success of the industry owes much to the Reynolds and the related Leethem families, through whose factories passed a number of men who later established enterprises of their own. The two families were particularly innovatory and were responsible for thirty-five of the fifty-nine patents taken out by Portsmouth corset-making firms between 1860 and 1899.

At the end of the century the largest corset factories were run by Leethem Reynolds in All Saints Road, by Charles Bayer in Regent Street, William Fletcher in Landport Street and Charles Leethem in Buckland Street. The Leethem Reynolds families owned five of the factories then working, including the Marina Factory in Highland Road, Southsea, opened in

George Cash, Regent Foundry, Aylward Street, Portsea. Despite the patenting of an innovative electric furnace in the 1960s, the foundry closed in 1972. The premises look unremarkable, but their legacy in the form of much of Portsmouth's street furniture is considerable. Photographed in 1973.

1897, in what was a new location, but nevertheless close to the grid of artisan houses, and therefore labour supply, in eastern Southsea. The corset industry did give rise to some support activities, such as the making of cardboard boxes and spring steel, which replaced the earlier whalebone, but the corset-making machinery came from other parts of the country. An intriguing question is why corset-making became so important in Portsmouth. The town was a specialist producer well before the introduction of factories, so the flair of the Reynolds and Leethems merely ensured that their industry remained important – they did not begin the specialisation. It is sometimes thought that the similarity with sail-making is an explanation, but it is more probable that the industry was built around the success of a few individuals who were then imitated by others. The proposition that whales would strand themselves on Whale Island, not built until the 1860s, providing a good supply of bone, can hardly be treated too seriously.

Some Portsmouth outfitters achieved a national reputation. Edwin and William Seagrove, whose shop and workshop was on the Hard, Portsea, described themselves in 1865 as 'by appointment to her Majesty'. Adverts for Totterdell & Co., Queen Street, were subtitled 'by appointment to Her Majesty's Royal Family'. Probably the best-known name is that of Gieve, later Gieves & Hawkes of Savile Row. James Gieve went into partnership with John Galt in 1852 with premises at 111 High Street. They seem to have been particularly resourceful, for during the Crimean War they hired a yacht and despatched it full of uniforms and tailors to Sebastopol. In 1904 Gieve merged with two other naval and military tailors, one of which was Seagrove, and moved operations to the Hard, where the shop and workshop, as Gieves & Hawkes, remained until 2001, when they moved to Gunwharf Quays. Some seventeen naval tailors alone are known to have existed during the nineteenth century, providing swords as well as uniforms. Of the non-specialist tailors, John Baker was the best known; he was mayor twice, Liberal MP between 1892 and 1900, received a knighthood, and had a gasworks locomotive named after him.

The corset industry may have possessed a good number of factories, but in relation to the numbers employed they were small. In contrast were the breweries, large structures with a modest workforce. Thus on the basis of rateable values in 1885, the six largest industrial premises in the town were breweries: Pike Spicer and Tessier in Penny Street, Jewell in Catherine Row, Portsea, Miles in King Street, Long in Hambrook Street and Lush in St George's Square. A notable local brewing name, Brickwood, is absent from the list, not because the firm did not exist, but because its growth came later. Founded in 1851, the business was expanded by the brothers Arthur and John, who in 1874 bought Long's Lord John Russell brewery in Commercial Road. In 1880 Bransbury's Hyde Park Road brewery was acquired, but seven years later they bought the substantial Tessier Brewery in Penny Street. Being unable to expand the site, Jewell's Brewery was purchased in 1899, and two years later it was the highest rated factory in Portsmouth. In 1910 the firm of Pike Spicer was acquired, making Brickwood far and away the largest player in the industry, with 245 tied houses. Sales of beer to the Victualling Board were limited, partly because of its poor keeping quality, but sales ashore were undoubtedly assisted by the presence of so many sailors and soldiers. In 1901 some 11,977 sailors and 2,490 soldiers swelled the market for beer. Brewing is no longer carried out in Portsmouth, the site of the last firm to remain, Brickwoods, having been converted to a car park, but there are some architecturally striking pubs still to be seen. These include: the Air Balloon in Commercial Road by A.H. Bone in 1888, the Talbot in Golsmith Avenue by A.E. Cogswell for Brickwood in 1896, the Rutland Hotel in Francis Avenue by A.E. Cogswell for Pike Spicer in 1898, the Graham Arms in George Street by A.E. Cogswell for Gibb in 1900 and the Devonshire Arms in Devonshire Avenue by J.J. Cotton for Long in 1906.

Some would argue that beer was an essential part of the diet (until fresh drinking water became generally available in the 1860s, this was probably true), but bread was certainly so. Flour milling by wind power gradually declined, leaving only New Dock Mill at work in 1913. The problem was twofold; cheap American grain could be milled at seaports to make flour at

A grid cover by George Cash, Regent Foundry. Mundane maybe, but this market provided a useful source of business for many Portsmouth ironfounders. The device in the centre is Portsmouth's 'Heaven's Light our Guide'. Photographed in 1976.

prices with which windmillers could not compete, and windmills could not be adapted to the use of high speed rollers which greatly reduced the cost of flour. More reliable than wind power was steam power, and in 1853 Landport Steam Mill opened in Lake Road, but it too closed in 1900. Baking, on the other hand, prospered. Some windmills had bakeries attached, but most bakeries were tiny, being located at the back of a shop; in 1847 there were seventy-eight bakeries in the town. Scott's bakery on the corner of Devonshire Avenue and Haslemere Road, which worked until the 1980s, was excellent example of the genre. Inevitably, some bakers were more dynamic than others and prospered; in this way Smith and Vosper in Green Road, and William Miller (Campion's after 1926) in Kent Street, who held the naval canteen contract at the end of the century, became large establishments. However, the largest bakery by a considerable margin was set up in the 1870s by the Portsea Island Cooperative Society. By 1901 it had grown at a startling pace to become the fifth largest factory in Portsmouth. Impetus to growth was much assisted by the building of a new bakery in Fratton Road in 1885, and by the production of pastry and confectionery from 1888.

As Portsmouth's population grew, so did the demand for gas lighting. Being unable to expand the Flathouse site, in 1872 the gas company built a decorative column-guided holder at nearby Rudmore. The introduction of the gas fire, the gas oven and the penny slot meter (consumers had to pay for their supply in advance, but a penny was perceived to be a small sum, thus encouraging sales and reducing bad debts), caused a dramatic increase in demand at the end of the century, output increasing by half between 1895 and 1904 alone, while the number of consumers trebled. This led to the construction of a new gasworks at Hilsea in 1905; the holders at this site may still be seen, but production ceased in 1968. Competing with gas for lighting was electricity, which was generated from 1894 at a small power station adjacent to the dry dock at the Camber. A crucial public utility was a system of sewage disposal, the absence of which had led to severe outbreaks of cholera. A drainage network was completed in 1868;

A lamp post by George Cash, Regent Foundry, in Barrack Street, now Peacock Lane, Old Portsmouth. 'Borough' of Portsmouth indicates that it predated 1926, when the town became a city. Photographed in 1976.

sewage flowed by gravity to a pumping station at Eastney, where it was lifted and moved to a holding tank which opened shortly after high tide. Additional steam pumps appeared in 1887 and in 1904 three huge gas engines came into operation. The distinctive, tall beam engine house of 1887 is now the centre of an industrial museum, where one of the beam engines is regularly steamed.

Portsmouth's railway system was laid down in the forty years after 1847 when the first terminus was opened in Commercial Road. The Board of Ordnance was initially unprepared to allow the Hilsea defences to be breached, forcing railway passengers to use the fine classical station built at Gosport by Sir William Tite in 1841. The present Commercial Road building, in high Victorian eclectic style, was finished in 1866, and the high level extension to Portsmouth Harbour followed in 1876. Fratton station was opened in 1885 as the main line link with the East Southsea Railway, which ran to Granada Road until its closure in 1914. The earliest remaining station is at Cosham, opened in 1848; it is much altered, but the original structure is not difficult to establish. Horse-drawn tramways made their appearance in 1865, electrification taking place in 1901, yet for a network which achieved considerable sophistication, little evidence remains. Sections of track have been preserved in Broad Street, Old Portsmouth, in Rugby Road and in Commercial Road, close to the Charles Dickens Museum.

Transport across the harbour was for centuries by wherry, but in 1840 the Floating Bridge Co. instituted a regular service by means of two steam-powered chain ferries. The Portsmouth landing point was Broad Street. The vessels, which were said to accommodate 500 passengers and twenty carriages, winched themselves along chains which were laid across the harbour. In the pre-motor age, these ferries saved what was a five-hour journey between Portsmouth and Gosport. Competition for passenger traffic was provided by the formation of the New Steam Launch Co. in 1884, resulting in considerable touting for trade; a joint service was agreed in 1888. Travel to and from the Isle of Wight was undertaken by small sailing ships until 1825 when the Portsmouth & Ryde Steam Packet Co. began a service using paddle steamers. By 1842 there were ten sailings each way in the summer months. Additional services were provided in 1850 by a small firm with two ships, but this was taken over by the Portsmouth & Ryde Co. the following year. In the early 1870s the Southsea & Isle of Wight Co., with four ships, sought a share of the traffic, but it was swallowed by the larger firm in 1877. Three years later the Portsmouth & Ryde Co. was bought by the railways; at this time there were nine vessels in the fleet, indicative of the rising importance of tourist traffic to the island. Shortly after this merger three new ships were bought; they were approximately 350 tons, the two largest being able to carry 550 passengers. Vehicle and animal traffic to and from the island was handled in idiosyncratic fashion by 'tow boats', small wooden boats whose broad stern doubled as a ramp, towed behind tugs. They are known to have been in operation by 1865, and somewhat surprisingly continued until the 1920s.

Piers are now associated with amusement rather than transport, but until the opening of the Harbour station and linked landing stage, they were vital for the Isle of Wight services. The first pier, Victoria, was opened in 1842 adjacent to the Square Tower in Old Portsmouth. The second, Royal Albert, dating from 1847, was specifically designed for the Isle of Wight steamers and was located near the later Harbour station landing stage; it was demolished in 1876 when the station opened. The third pier, Clarence, was used as a point of call by the Isle of Wight ships from its inauguration in 1861 and was linked to the Town station by horse tram in 1866. The fourth pier, South Parade, completed in 1879, was also a point of call, and it was in an effort to generate more traffic that the East Southsea Railway was created, its terminus being only 300m from the pier. It was destroyed by fire in 1904 and rebuilt in 1908.

It will be apparent from this review of the industries of the town, that apart from clothing, manufacturing outside the dockyard was largely restricted to supplying the population with food, drink, iron goods, and gas. One result was that not many substantial fortunes were made and the town did not spawn a large middle class. Those who might be so classified were mostly naval and military officers. It is surely no accident that there is in Portsmouth a notable absence of large houses and surrounding estates so frequently found on the fringes of industrial towns fashioned in the nineteenth century. There are no parks created from the gardens of the rich and no university endowed by philanthropically-minded industrialists.

Left: A lamp post by W.H. Sperring, Landport, in Campbell Road, Southsea, dated 1907. The hinged door indicates that it was an electric lamp. Photographed in 1979.

Below: A manhole cover by Garnett & Co., Ferrumite Works. This one is in King's Terrace, built in the 1820s, when houses had cellars beneath the pavement; coal merchants would lift the cover and deliver the coal. Photographed in 1981.

Right: Maurice Ablitt & Son, Nancy Road, Fratton. The works was established on this site in 1908 as motor coach and shoeing smiths, an interesting link between what are now thought to be quite different forms of transport. Photographed in 1975.

Below: Thomas Barnes, Warblington Street, Old Portsmouth. Like many small metalworking firms, Barnes had two small forges and a variety of equipment for shaping and cutting metal and wire. The works closed in the 1950s and was eventually replaced by housing. Photographed in 1969.

Left: Thomas Barnes, Warblington Street, Old Portsmouth. The photograph shows a tyre oven, in which the metal tyre for wooden wheels was heated to make it expand. The hot tyre was then fitted to the wheel on a metal tyre plate and quickly doused with water, cooling and contracting the tyre onto the wheel. By the 1950s there can hardly have been much demand for such metal tyres. Photographed in 1969.

Below: McKinley Engineering Works, Mile End. To the uninformed the view shown suggests clutter and a lack of organisation, but such was fairly typical of many small engineering firms. To overcome the weakness of the building, a separate internal frame was constructed on to which heavy items could be placed. Photographed in 1983.

William Treadgold, Bishop Street, Portsea. The firm were small general metalworkers, unusual in having a shop attached. It was the shop, which sold a variety of metal goods, which caused the firm to linger on until 1988. Photographed in 1973.

William Treadgold, Bishop Street, Portsea. A view of the general workshop not long before it ceased working. The premises are now a museum and the workshop remains very much as it was. Photographed in 1978.

Daufman Tailors, Queen Street, Portsea. This firm was one of the larger tailors, and one of the longest-lived, occupying the premises shown in 1914; by the mid-1970s only a handful of naval tailors remained. They made good use of their tall premises for advertising their presence. Photographed in 1973.

Right: Voller's Corset Workshop, Fratton Road. Corset-making was a labour-intensive activity, none more so than the punching of eyelets, achieved here by two manual, pedal assisted machines. The workshop was associated with a medium-sized clothing shop, which possibly helped the continuation of corset production. Photographed in 1983.

Below: Voller's Corset Workshop, Fratton Road. The workshop employed only a dozen or so women, and is to be seen immediately to the right of the shop. Photographed in 1976.

Opposite top: William Treadgold, Bishop Street, Portsea, The shop with a small section of the hundreds of boxes containing an enormous range of nuts, bolts, screws, nails, hinges and the like. Photographed in 1978.

Leethem's Marina Corset Factory, Highland Road, Southsea. Corset factories were normally functional buildings, but at least this one, opened in 1897, was enlivened by the attempt to use as much natural light as possible through clerestory windows in the roof. Photographed in 1976.

A part of Long's Brewery, Hambrook Street, Southsea, 1898. One of the last and unusually ornate elements of the brewery shortly before its demolition in 1967. The stone setts making up the road add to the feel of times past.

Long's Brewery store, Hambrook Street. Enough of the decorative store remains to suggest that it was the work of the firm's in-house architect J.J. Cotton, whose trademark was stone string courses (see his Devonshire Arms pub below). Photographed in 1972.

Brickwood's Brewery, Admiralty Road, Portsea. The roadway was formerly a public thoroughfare, Daniel Street, which was bought by the firm and absorbed into the brewery, as was the church – the buff coloured building with a pediment. Photographed in 1978.

Brickwood's Brewery, Admiralty Road. To save fuel the wort – beer at an early stage – was run into a receiver, hence the letters 'WR', located above the copper, in which the wort was boiled with hops. Photographed in 1978.

Staff house, Brickwood's Brewery. It was said that the inverted roof of this staff house on brewery premises was to collect rainwater for domestic use. Perhaps there was indeed a shortage of water on site. Photographed in 1978.

Young's Victory Brewery, Thomas Street, Landport. This was a medium-sized brewery acquired by Friary Meux in 1959 and promptly closed. The premises were then used for other purposes until the early 1990s. Photographed in 1970.

Whitbread's bottling store, St Nicholas Street, Old Portsmouth, 1912. By the end of the nineteenth century some breweries were large enough to establish depots in other towns. Whitbread was to become the last brewery in Portsmouth after it took over Brickwood in 1971. Photographed in 1976.

Air Balloon, Commercial Road, 1888. The name derives from an air balloon which ascended from the site. The designer, Alfred Bone, was a Portsmouth architect who is better known for his schools than his pubs, but here he makes good use of pargetting – decorative mortar within a timber frame – knapped flints and wooden porches to create a very distinctive pub. Photographed in 1983.

Talbot, Golsmith Avenue, 1896. Arthur Edward Cogswell, Portsmouth's best-known pub architect, at his peak, incorporating a 'witch's hat' above the corner tower, elaborate half-timbering and elongated keystones on the ground floor. In the pre-motor age, note the coach entrance on the left. Photographed in 1983.

Rutland Arms, Francis Avenue, 1898. Regarded by many as his best work, this Cogswell pub is one of his half-timbered examples, but has oriel windows and the tower cap is muted compared with his more common 'witch's hat' design. Photographed in 1983.

Devonshire Arms, Devonshire Avenue, 1906. Some breweries employed an in-house architect; this is the product of J.J. Cotton who worked for Long's, whose trademark was stone string courses, even in the dormer window surrounds. Photographed in 1983.

Graham Arms, George Street, 1900. One of Cogswell's more unusual designs, seeking to make the best out of a small site by tall first floor windows with exploded pediments and substantial gables above. Note the column supporting the first floor in front of the corner door. Photographed in 1983.

Scott's bakery, Devonshire Avenue. One of the many small bakeries with a shop at the front which prospered until the inter-war years. Occupying premises obviously built as a house, dating from the 1890s, the firm continued into the 1980s. Photographed in 1976.

Robert Taubman & Sons, Princes Street, Mile End. This unimpressive building, once surrounded by housing, was home to one of the more unusual branches of the food industry – tripe dressing. It had ceased production when the photograph was taken in 1972.

Tannery, Chapel Street, Southsea, 1840s. It may seem incongruous now to find small factories in the middle of dense housing, especially a tannery which would give off distinctive smells, but that was the nature of the Victorian town. The typical ventilation louvres on the upper floor indentify the factory, to the right. The site is now housing. Photographed in 1972.

Rudmore gasholder, 1872. Growing demand, and space restrictions at their Flathouse site, caused the Portsea Island Gaslight & Coke Co. to build a holder at Rudmore. It was originally a two-lift structure, and was masked from the residents of Commercial Road by an arched wall. Subsequently a third lift was added, making the ironwork, and when full, the tank itself protrude above the wall. Demolished to make way for the continental ferry port in 1976. Photographed in 1970.

Hilsea gasworks, 1905. In place of the traditional horizontal retorts, in 1925 a vertical retort house, in which the downward movement of coal was continuous, was added. The tall building was a landmark on the north-east of Portsea Island. It was closed in 1968. Photographed in 1968.

Hilsea gasworks. In order to deliver coal to the top of the new vertical retorts, an inclined railway was constructed and coal wagons were emptied by tipping them over in a machine made by Babcock & Wilcox. Photographed in 1926.

Hilsea gasworks. To facilitate the movement of materials about the site, an overhead monorail was constructed. It was one of the largest ever built in the UK. Photographed in 1968.

Sewage pumping station, Henderson Road, Eastney, 1867. The small engine house contained steam beam engines by Clayton of Preston, which pumped sewage into a holding tank, periodically emptied into the sea. This was Portsmouth's first drainage system. Photographed in 1978.

Sewage pumping station, Simpson Road, Stamshaw, 1886. As the town expanded, so did the sewage and rainwater drainage system, and additional auxiliary pumping stations were required to lift into the original network. Photographed in 1973.

Sewage pumping station, Henderson Road, 1887. Population growth resulted in the need for further drainage capacity. This was achieved through the installation of two large beam engines by James Watt in the typically tall and decorative building on the right. Photographed in 1971.

Sewage pumping station, Copnor, 1909. Another auxiliary facility keeping pace with suburban population growth. Photographed in 1984.

Cosham railway station, 1848. The terminus at Portsmouth was opened in 1847, but was rebuilt in 1866, making Cosham the oldest remaining station. It was built for the London & South Western Railway in cottage orné style; there are some neat hood moulds above the windows of the left. The platform canopy has since been greatly shortened. Photographed in 1970.

Green Lanes signal box. The interior of a manually-operated signal box. The wheel was for the operation of the level crossing gates which controlled access to Hilsea gasworks. The box was removed in 1972. Photographed in 1971.

Portsmouth high level station, 1876. In 1976 the platform canopy at the western end of the station was shortened, revealing the ironwork. The letters 'PWER', that is, Portsmouth Waterside Extension Railway, were worked into the roof brackets.

Portsmouth high level station, 1876. The station was rebuilt in 1988.

East Southsea railway station, 1885. In the expectation of considerable traffic a fairly large station was built in Granada Road, close to South Parade Pier. Optimism proved to be unfounded and the line closed in 1914, the station building becoming a garage. There are now houses on the site. Photographed in 1971.

East Southsea station, 1885. This interior shot taken in 1971 shows the ironwork of the original train shed. Provision was made for four platforms in the hope that passengers would use the line to reach the Isle of Wight via South Parade Pier.

Railway Buildings, Fratton, 1902. The joint railway companies erected two blocks of flats for their employees adjacent to Fratton station; the initials of the companies (LSWR and LBSCR) may be discerned at the head of the entrance pillars. Photographed in 1977.

Right: Wash houses, Railway Buildings, Fratton, 1902. Each of the two blocks of flats had its own, fairly substantial semi-circular wash house. They were demolished in 1986 and the flats refurbished. Photographed in 1986.

Middle: Bishop's Quay, Wharf Road, Rudmore. Vessels at Bishop's Quay probably had to bottom in the mud for loading and unloading, but it is clear that a short, narrow gauge railway track (2ft 3in) was employed to move goods to and from the shore. Photographed in 1972.

Bottom: South Parade Pier, 1879, rebuilt 1908. The first pier, which was privately owned, was destroyed by fire in 1904. Recognising the value of the amenity, the Corporation put up the money for a replacement, to the design of the local architect C.W. Ball. Photographed in 2002.

Four

The Twentieth Century after 1913

Many see the twentieth century in Portsmouth as one of industrial decline as the heady days of *Dreadnought* building faded away and as the dockyard began to lose its central position in the town. Change there certainly was, but in fact until the 1960s it was not really fundamental, giving the inter-war years and the immediate post-Second World War era considerable similarity to what had gone before. Subsequently, however, the evolving view of the Navy's role in defence, and the reorganisation of the manufacturing industry in Britain and elsewhere ensured that there were substantial differences between 1960 and 2000.

In the dockyard, the rearmament building programme, which had seen the number of warships launched each year fall while the total tonnage launched rose, effectively finished once war was declared. The last two capital ships to be launched in the yard, *Queen Elizabeth* in 1914 and *Royal Sovereign* in 1915, were laid down before hostilities began. For the remainder of the war years, the dockyard reverted to its repair and refit function, construction work being relegated to the building of submarines, relatively small craft. The first two, J1 and J2, were actually built in the same dock, itself an indication of their size, which was 1,179 tons. Three K class submarines of 1,780 tons then followed. During the war 2,410 vessels were refitted, 1,784 ships were docked, major repairs were effected on sixteen large warships, torpedo bulges and improved armour plating were fitted to a number of ships following the deficiencies exposed at the Battle of Jutland, and armaments were installed in hundreds of merchant ships. Not surprisingly the workforce increased to 23,000. Among these were women who, because of the shortage of men, found themselves undertaking tasks in boathouses, engineering shops and in the foundry, in addition to jobs where physical strength was not at such a premium. By 1917 about 1,750 'triangle girls', so called because of their identifying badge, were at work in the yard. Unfortunately entrenched attitudes ensured that they lost their jobs at the end of the war.

As had occurred at the end of wars in the past, in 1919 there was an immediate cut back in the yard workforce, a process given momentum by the disarmament agreement signed in Washington in 1922. By the mid-1920s only 8,000 remained, although it should be said that by reducing the working week by seven hours in 1921, about 1,000 men who had been discharged

Victory shortly after her final docking in 1922, the chimneys of the Smithery in the distance.

were re-employed. The changes were reflected in construction work. The 9,750-ton cruiser *Effingham*, which had been laid down in 1917, left the slip in 1921, the first launch since the K class submarines had been completed four years earlier. There was then a gap of five years before the cruisers *Suffolk* and *London* left the stocks in 1926 and 1927 respectively. An event which was to have important consequences for heritage tourism later in the century, took place in 1922 when Nelson's flagship *Victory* was moved from the harbour into one of Bentham's docks, No.2. She has remained a serving ship of the Navy and this has ensured the flow of funds needed for the never-ending repair work necessary for a ship of her age. Not too distant from *Victory* in the oldest part of the yard, a new Semaphore Tower was completed in 1930, replacing the original destroyed by fire in 1913. In a most imaginative stroke, Lion Gate, which had stood in Queen Street near the present Lion Terrace until the Portsea fortifications were removed in the 1870s, was rebuilt beneath the Tower. Unfortunately this impressive monument faces seawards and cannot be seen by the visitor to the Heritage Area. During the 1930s a number of small craft were built, and it was not until 1933 with the launch of the cruisers *Neptune*, followed by *Amphion* and *Aurora* in 1934, that major construction took place. During the later 1930s there was extensive rebuilding of battleships such as *Repulse*, *Warspite*, *Renown* and *Queen Elizabeth*, and the conversion of light cruisers to anti-aircraft ships, all contributing to an increase in dockyard employment to the 1914 level.

During the Second World War one ship, the cruiser *Sirius*, was completed in 1942, but she had been laid down before the war. With a curious similarity to 1914-18, the principal construction work during the war concerned submarines, two of which, *Tireless* and *Token*, were launched in 1945. The proximity of France, making the yard vulnerable to German air attack, caused the larger warships to avoid Portsmouth, but this did not prevent the yard from making a major contribution to the preparations for D-Day from 1943 onwards. Many of the docks became crammed with landing craft of various kinds, while work on the Mulberry Harbour system was undertaken. It was labour-intensive work; at its peak some 25,000 were employed in the yard.

For once, the ending of the war did not lead to wholesale redundancies, for in place of conventional hostilities came the Cold War. What did cause the beginning of long-term contraction were fundamental changes in the way war at sea was prosecuted. Nuclear submarines armed with intercontinental ballistic missiles, and a relatively small number of medium-sized warships with great strike power, came to form the basis of the Navy in the 1960s. Thus only five frigates – *Leopard* (1951), *Rhyl* (1959), *Nubian* (1960), *Sirius* (1964), and *Andromeda* (1967) – were built after the war, the last-named ending four and a half centuries of naval shipbuilding at Portsmouth. Further evidence of the new emphasis was the presence of some 2,000 scientific staff at the Admiralty Surface Weapons Establishment (later Defence Evaluation and Research Agency) on Portsdown Hill, not in the dockyard. The Defence Review of 1981 recommended that only two main naval bases were required. Plymouth and Rosyth were selected, Chatham was closed, and Portsmouth was relegated to a maintenance and repair role, simultaneously losing the title 'Dockyard', officially closing in March 1984. Preparations for the Falklands War in 1982 brought a brief stay of execution, but the workforce, which had stood at 8,000 in 1981, soon fell to 2,800. At the same time the yard was privatised.

Not only was there fundamental change in the nature of the Navy, but also most of the buildings and docks in the oldest part of the dockyard shifted from naval to tourist use. In 1985 ownership of many of the buildings was transferred from the Ministry of Defence to the Portsmouth Naval Base Property Trust (PT), with a brief to maintain the historic buildings in its care; it received £6 million from the Ministry to commence operations. To ensure an income the PT rents its premises, most of which are used by the tourist industry. For some years the ground floor of No.9 Store was used as a café, while the ground floor of No.10 Store and the whole of No.11 Store are part of the Victory museum. No.5 Boathouse houses the *Mary Rose* Museum, No.6 Boathouse is host to the Action Stations activities centre, on the top floor is the Institute of Maritime and Heritage Studies of Portsmouth University, and No.7 Boathouse has a café and a shop, together with the Dockyard Apprentice Museum. Opposite these last three buildings is the very different No.4 Boathouse, finished in 1939, and the only one of its kind in the yard; a collection of small boats is maintained here, and from to time exhibitions run by the PT are staged. The PT also owns the historically-important Block Mills, but they are outside the boundary of the Heritage Area, and lie empty and in a parlous condition. The block making machinery has been dispersed, save for a circular saw which is built into the structure. In Bentham's No.1 Dock lies M33, a First World War monitor or gunboat, owned by Hampshire County Council; in No.2 is *Victory*, and in No.3 *Mary Rose*. Only *Warrior* does not occupy a

The Coppersmiths Shop, 1929. Architecturally certainly inter-war.

Some idea of the ceremony associated with the passage of dignitaries is captured in this photograph of the train carrying the Prince of Wales leaving the Royal Shelter in 1935.

position inside the dockyard. The warship was Britain's first ironclad, launched on the Thames in 1860, and in Portsmouth since June 1987. By any standards this is an important tourist complex, and is visited by 750,000 people annually.

The numbers employed in the dockyard in the inter-war period may have fluctuated according to the political situation, but the yard's position with regard to the industries of the town remained dominant, slightly less than half Portsmouth's industrial workforce finding employment there in both 1921 and 1931. What did change, however, was the clothing industry's share of total employment, for no longer did it rival the dockyard. In 1921 clothing accounted for only a quarter of manufacturing labour, and this had fallen further to a fifth by 1931. This general trend was continued after the war, as dockyard employment ran ahead to account for just over half the total industrial jobs in 1951, while clothing contracted to a mere tenth. Ten years later rationalisation in the dockyard had caused its share to drop to two-fifths, but it remained well ahead of clothing manufacture, confirming that Portsmouth's traditional dual economy no longer existed. Three other manufacturing sectors were, in 1961, almost as important as clothing, as the economy diversified and began to take up a profile closer to that in many other towns. Mechanical engineering had existed for many decades, but rather on a small-scale jobbing basis; now national firms were attracted to the Portsmouth industrial estates by low wages and the availability of premises in south-east England. The manufacture of electrical goods was a relatively new activity, attracted to Portsmouth for the same reasons as mechanical engineering. The third industry was aircraft production, which had received a considerable boost during the war. It was noticeable that the new arrivals did not take the place of the old firms in historic areas of the city, but were located on peripheral industrial estates, as a result of planning policy, giving Old Portsmouth, for instance, a quite different ambience. By the 1960s it was almost wholly residential, when once it had been a mix of many different activities.

Despite the contraction in the clothing sector, the inter-war period witnessed scant change in the old established industries. However, many premises were lost in the war for they were located in Old Portsmouth, Portsea and Landport, the areas closest to the dockyard, the target of German bombers. Those surviving continued in their traditional fashion since demand was buoyant in the 1950s as the economy was rebuilt. However, the 1960s and early 1970s saw the terminal decline of most of the traditional industries. They were victim of what was termed 'de-industrialisation', as the advantages of large factories not located in inner city areas became clear, and as countries with distinctly lower labour costs were able to underprice many British products. Small engineering works such as Thatcher in Oyster Street, Old Portsmouth, and McKinley at Mile End, were lost as a result. Only three of the eleven iron founders working in the late 1930s survived the war: W.H. Sperring in Clarendon Street, Landport, George Cash in Aylward Street, Portsea, and Robert Wood in Warblington Street, Old Portsmouth. But all three had closed by 1973. It should be said that an additional reason for the closure of Sperring was the compulsory purchase of the site by the Council for a housing scheme. The small shipyards at Mile End disappeared, leaving Vosper at the Camber as the residual firm, drawing its success from the specialised manufacture of torpedo boats and fast craft for the British and foreign navies. Hampered by the cramped situation the firm, now Vosper-Thornycroft, closed their Camber yard in 1987, and concentrated production at their new, covered facility at Portchester. The Council-owned dry dock at the Camber survived the First World War; one of the last tasks undertaken was the rebuilding of Captain Scott's *Discovery* in 1925. The following year the dock lost its repair function when it was modified, and in 1928 became the dock for colliers supplying the adjacent power station.

Because the corset industry had been put on a factory basis and had established worldwide markets, it fared better than the clothing industry as a whole in the 1920s and 1930s. In fact Weingarten Brothers opened a new factory in Goldsmith Avenue in 1922, now converted to flats. There was one casualty, the spring steel factory at Mile End, which was sold in 1924 to Smith's for the manufacture of crisps. Two of Leethem's factories, the Sultan in Buckland Street, and the Arundel in Landport Street, were lost in air raids, as were three others in Telegraph Street, Common Street, and St Mary's Road. A further change was Leethem's decision to open a new factory at Farlington in 1949, but the decline in demand for corsets meant that it was necessary to enter the very competitive underwear market; indeed, in 1958 500 employees were placed on short time. In 1971 there were still nine factories which included corset-making in their repertoire, but there was a spate of closures in the following decade, leaving Voller in Fratton Road, employing only a handful of people, as the sole representative of this once important industry. At least some of the premises remain, the best example being the Marina Factory in Highland Road.

In contrast, there is now no physical evidence of brewing in Portsmouth, the four breweries that survived the First World War having been demolished. Long in Hambrook Street ceased brewing in 1934, the Victory Brewery in Thomas Street, Landport, worked until 1959, the Elm Brewery in King Street closed in 1962, and finally Brickwood (then owned by Whitbread) in Admiralty Road shut in 1983. These changes were not so much due to falling demand as the result of mergers to which the industry was prone. Brickwood acquired seven breweries in the late 1920s and early 1930s, and then in 1953 bought Portsmouth United Breweries' Elm Brewery. In 1971 Brickwood was itself acquired by Whitbread. Acquisition sometimes resulted in closure, but not of the tied pubs that went with the merger. Thus, immediately after its purchase by Friary Meux in 1959, the Victory Brewery was closed. As a coda it is worth adding that Portsmouth's best-known pub architect, A.E. Cogswell, continued working in the 1920s, producing for instance the Ship Anson on the Hard, the Florist on Fratton Road, and the Coach and Horses on London Road.

This sorry tale of de-industrialisation applied equally to two of the public utilities, despite increasing demand from consumers. At the Hilsea gasworks a large additional retort house was completed in 1925, but in the mid-1960s the advent of natural gas from the North Sea removed

The bleak environment which was the Pay Office where the weekly packet were made up. (PRDHT)

the justification for coal gas; the works at Flathouse and Hilsea were therefore closed in 1968, although the holders at Hilsea were retained. The original electric power station at the Camber was replaced between 1946 and 1951 by a very much larger red brick structure with two towering chimneys which dominated the Old Portsmouth skyline; it was the largest industrial building ever constructed in Portsmouth. Nationalisation in 1948 meant that the station came to be in competition with much larger plants with lower costs. Output was cut back after 1965 and the station was closed in 1977; it is now a car park.

In the field of rail transport the principal changes effected were the transfer of the goods depot from the Town station to Fratton in 1936, electrification in 1937, the rebuilding of the Harbour station in 1937-38, and the end of steam in 1967. In the 1930s a new form of transport came to Portsmouth: air travel. All credit to them, the City Council (Portsmouth became a City in 1926) decided that a municipally-run airport was justified, and spent a considerable sum blowing up old fortifications and reclaiming land in the north-eastern part of Portsea Island. The airport opened in 1932, and services to Ryde and then other towns in Britain were inaugurated. As early as 1934 some 20,000 passengers were using the airport, and a service to Paris began. In 1937 the aircraft manufacturer Airspeed, which later merged with de Havilland, famous for the first commercial jet, the Comet, relocated its operations from York, creating 600 jobs at the airport, and helping to diversify the economy. However, in 1945 the Council rejected a scheme to extend the runways to take bigger aircraft, so the old grass runways remained in use. Channel Airways began operations in 1955, and although 63,000 passengers passed through in 1966, the short, grass runways gave aircraft little margin for error. Almost inevitably, a wet surface, which made braking difficult, caused not one, but two aircraft on the very same day in 1967 to land and end up outside the airport boundary. There were no fatalities, but it was effectively the end of the airport, which eventually became a housing estate.

The volume of passenger traffic across the harbour between Portsmouth and Gosport proved attractive to investors, so that in 1930 three companies were vying with each other: the Gosport & Portsea Steam Launch Co., the Port of Portsmouth Steam Launch & Towing Co., and the

Port of Portsmouth Floating Bridge & Steam Launch Co. Between them they possessed twelve vessels, ten of which were small craft between forty-six tons and seventy-nine tons, the other two being the floating bridges of 400 tons. The latter carried 71,521 vehicles in 1951-52, but shortly after were hard hit by the end of petrol rationing, which, together with increased tariffs, caused many Portsmouth firms to use the longer road route. The company ceased working in 1959. In 1961 the other two operators amalgamated to form the Portsmouth Harbour Ferry Co., which inherited four steam and three diesel vessels. From 1966 the service was worked by the *Gosport Queen* and the *Portsmouth Queen*, which can take 250 passengers, and are substantially more efficient than their predecessors. Quite apart from their variable thrust propellers making them very manoeuvrable, they have covered accommodation which earlier ferries lacked.

The tradition of employing paddle steamers on the Isle of Wight run established in the nineteenth century continued in the twentieth; when the ships were transferred to Southern Railways in 1923, all five were paddlers. When they were replaced in the late 1920s and 1930s, once again paddlers were preferred, although they were much larger vessels. The *Duchess of Norfolk*, replaced in 1937, was 381 tons, but *Sandown*, which came into service in 1934, was 684 tons, while *Southsea* and *Whippingham*, bought in 1930, were both 825 tons. *Ryde*, which began work in 1937, and outlived all the other paddlers, was slightly smaller at 603 tons. Their tonnage was reflected in the number of passengers they could carry: *Ryde's* capacity was 1,011, but both *Southsea* and *Whippingham* were registered to take 1,183. Southern Railways' policy of employing bigger boats derived from the enormous demand for travel to and from the Isle of Wight in the inter-war era, no less than two million people making the journey in 1927. After the war the balance moved in favour of diesel-powered propeller ships such as *Brading* and *Southsea* (the *Southsea* referred to above was sunk in 1941), which came into service in 1948, and the later *Shanklin*. Technology moved on, and when the next generation of vessels made its appearance in 1985, they were catamarans, capable of twice the speed of the ships they replaced. By this time tourist demand had fallen dramatically, making the smaller 'cats', with a capacity of 406 passengers, perfectly suited to the crossing. Technologically fascinating, but of rather less significance in respect of passengers carried, was the hovercraft service to Ryde from Southsea beach, which began in 1965; the craft currently on the run can seat ninety-six passengers.

By the 1920s freight traffic to the Isle of Wight was such that it had outgrown the capacity of the primitive tow boats, causing Southern Railways to introduce a purpose-built car ferry service to Fishbourne in 1927. The first vessel, *Fishbourne*, which worked until 1961, was equipped with

Launched at Portsmouth in 1931, *Nightingale* was a mining tender for HMS *Vernon*. *(PRDHT)*

No.4 Boathouse, for the maintenance of small craft, was begun in the late 1930s, but work was suspended at the outbreak of war and it was never finished. It was to have extended to the right in the picture. The boathouse entrance is at the bottom right, and bottom left is the canal leading into the mast pond. Photographed in 1973.

double twin screws, that is, two facing aft and two facing forward, making turning unnecessary. She was diesel powered and could carry eighteen cars. She was joined by *Wootton* the following year, and as an indication of the build-up of traffic, *Hilsea* in 1930. Between September 1938 and September 1939 some 12,793 cars and 1,633 lorries travelled to and from the island. Unlike passenger traffic, in the 1950s and 1960s vehicular traffic continued to increase, and summer weekends saw the introduction of twenty-four-hour working from a new terminal at Broad Street at the Camber. From 1973 a class of larger, 761-ton ferries, *Caedmon*, *Centred*, *Cenwulf*, and *Cuthred*, was introduced. However, the facility became inadequate, and with the demolition of the power station the Camber dock was filled in and in 1982 became the ferry car park; a new ramp was constructed for the ferries. Continued demand prompted the purchase of even larger ferries: the 2,036-ton *St Catherine* in 1983, followed by *St Helen*, *St Cecilia*, *St Faith* and *St Clare*, all of which were only marginally less than 3,000 tons.

A new, international dimension was added to the harbour facilities in 1976, when a municipally-owned continental ferry port was opened on the site of the Rudmore gasholder. It dwarfed the earlier initiatives by the city, namely the tiny quay at Flathouse dating from 1921, and the nearby Albert Johnson Quay opened in 1968, which deals with conventional freight and containers. The City Council's Transportation Committee was convinced that the rise in the number of people holidaying abroad by car was likely to continue, that union problems at Southampton would greatly reduce competition from this quarter, and that Portsmouth's location gave advantages to those making for much of France and Spain. The Council accepted the proposal, and was pleased to find that St Malo had already decided to go ahead with a ferry terminal of their own, thus complementing Portsmouth's plan. The termination of the M275 at the ferry port, the sailing time to France saved by comparison with Southampton, and the agreement of the Ministry of Defence, which felt that the ferries would not impair the much-reduced naval movements in the harbour, were additional benefits. The work on the terminal took only 300 days to complete, the emphasis in the first instance being placed on dredging,

A satirical view of events on pay day, which for many years took place in the dockyardmen's own time. (*PRDHT*)

loading ramps and parking space rather than on the terminal buildings, which were regarded as temporary. By 1979 almost one million passengers were handled, and almost overnight Portsmouth became the country's second largest passenger port after Dover. Expansion followed; two million passengers passed through in 1987 and three million in 1994. Freight services have performed similarly. There are now four link spans or berths which can be used simultaneously.

As traffic has risen so has the size of ferries. Brittany Ferries, which have used the terminal since its inauguration, initially employed vessels such as *Quiberon*, 11,831 tons, with a capacity of 1,402 passenger and 260 cars, and from 1978, *Duc du Normandie*, 13,000 tons. Just over a decade later, *Bretagne*, 23,000 tons, capable of carrying 2,056 passengers and 580 cars, and in 1992, *Normandie*, 27,541 tons, which could take 2,123 passengers and 600 cars, were in service. Similarly, Townsend-Thoresen, which was taken over by P&O in 1987, ran vessels of comparable size, although two of their original ferries, *Pride of Hampshire* and *Pride of Cherbourg*, were 14,760 tons. *Pride of Portsmouth* and *Pride of Le Havre*, both introduced in 1994, were 33,336 tons, while the slightly earlier *Pride of Bilbao*, 1993, was 37,583 tons. The latter ship has a capacity of 2,563 passengers and 600 cars. These new ferries were a response to the growth in demand from tourists, but also important was the space requirement of facilities such as a variety of restaurants, bars, shops and cinemas (*Pride of Bilbao* even has a swimming pool) introduced by the ferry companies to meet competition provided by the Channel Tunnel. The most recent ferries may not be as long as the warships of the *Dreadnought* class, but their height and bright paintwork nevertheless make an impressive sight. For centuries naval vessels dominated the port, and it is a remarkable coincidence that as the dockyard has lost much of its significance, so really large commercial vessels have made their appearance. The ferry terminal is also used by P&O's *Portsmouth Express*, a catamaran which can carry 868 passengers and 225 cars and which began the run to Cherbourg in 2000; it halves the crossing time, although it is withdrawn in rough weather. Commodore Shipping operates a freight service from the terminal to the Channel islands, using the relatively small *Commodore Goodwill* and *Commodore Clipper*.

A floating crane coming into dock. These cranes were especially useful since they could easily be moved round the dockyard as required. *(PRDHT)*

A cruiser in the dockyard with workers tidying up the jetty in the foreground. *(Drawing by John Green, 2000)*

Left: The 'dockies', not 'dockers', was the name given to the dockyardmen. The drawing by John Green lists some forty-five trades to be found in the yard.

Right: A graphite drawing of a dockie with tool and lunch bags, by John Green.

Left: An impression of a rigger's mate, heavily laden with the tools of his trade, which he had to carry with him to vessels wherever they were berthed in the dockyard. Riggers looked after wire and fibre ropes both on ships and in the yard in general. *(Drawing by John Green)*

Right: Images of the dockyard, 1937-1982. The iron horse refers to the steam locomotives which took the place of horses on the dockyard transport system. The cyclists represent the many thousand dockyard workers who cycled to work, making an impressive sight at the end of the working day. (*Drawing by John Green*)

Below: Making safety nets in the Rigging Loft. (*PRDHT*)

A testimony to the manoeuvrability of paddlers was their use as dockyard tugs. Photographed in 1970.

Working the sluice gate mechanism of a dock. By tradition the officer in charge was always accompanied by his dog, top left. (*Drawn by John Green*)

A destroyer being docked. (*Drawn by John Green*)

Ceylon in Portsmouth in 1960. (*Drawn by John Green*)

Sirius leaves No.5 slip in 1964, the penultimate ship to be built at Portsmouth Dockyard. *(PRDHT)*

The delicate work of refitting armament for *Bristol*. Apart from the size of the gun, a notable feature is the near absence of workers. *(PRDHT)*

Right: Tartar leaving Portsmouth to join the reserve fleet in 1980. The length of the paying-off pennant is proportionate to the ship's service. *(PRDHT)*

Left: An imposing aircraft carrier alongside a smaller ship. *(Artist John Green)*

Below: Sir Tristram, repaired after damage sustained in the Falklands War sailing into Portsmouth Harbour. *(PRDHT)*

Hosemakers on the top floor of the Steam Factory, later No.2. Ship Shop. Photographed in 1983.

An array of minesweepers in No.2 Basin against the backdrop of the Steam Factory in 1986. In the foreground is *Wotton*, and behind is *Hubberston*. *(PRDHT)*

An impression of a cruiser in dock. The self-propelled steam crane, the rudimentary crane with a simple jib and the 250-ton crane in the background together make an interesting group of contrasting technologies. (*Drawn by John Green*)

Left: Minesweeper *Iveston* in No.8 Dock, with No.2 Basin and the Steam Factory in the background. Photographed in 1985. (*PRDHT*)

Below: A cruiser in No.15 Dock with many dockies in evidence. (*Artist John Green*)

A modern destroyer, *York*, completed in 1980, photographed in No.15 Dock in 1992. *(PRDHT)*

Two motor torpedo boats, *Brave Borderer* (nearest camera) and *Brave Swordsman*, built in 1960 by Vospers.

Caisson Gate, Camber dock, Old Portsmouth. The caisson was installed when the entrance was rebuilt in 1927-28 to accommodate colliers supplying the power station. The caisson is partly raised, causing its ends to be above the level of the quay. Photographed in 1972.

Camber Dock, Old Portsmouth. The covered ways holding conveyor belts taking coal to the power station may be seen in this photograph taken in 1971.

Left: Camber Dock, Old Portsmouth. A view of the cranes which unloaded colliers in the dock. Photographed in 1972.

Below: Camber Dock, Old Portsmouth. Detail of the 5-ton electric coal dock cranes by Babcock & Wiccox. On the right is the submarine escape tower for training submariners in HMS *Vernon*. Photographed in 1972.

Right: Ship Anson, Hard, 1923. A rebuild by Cogswell's son, Victor, photographed in 1984.

Left: Florist, Fratton Road, 1923. This was a rebuild of an earlier pub; brewers liked to change the face of their properties to encourage customers. This is by A.E. Cogswell, half-timbered with a notable 'witch's hat'. Photographed in 1983.

Ship Anson, Hard, detail. Almost all Brickwood's pubs had the name of the brewery fashioned in terrazzo work. The background to the name made use of a variety of colours to give an overall pink effect. This ingenious touch has now been removed from all the firm's pubs. Photographed in 1984.

Coach and Horses, London Road, 1929. A rebuild by Cogswell of an earlier pub. The somewhat military flavour reflects the nearby Hilsea fortifications. Photographed in 1983.

Scott's bakery roundsman. Very much part of the Southsea scene for many years, the roundsman delivered the firm's products to customers, and was conceivably one reason why such a small firm lasted for so long. Photographed in 1976.

OEC Motor Cycles, Atlanta Works, Stamshaw Road. In the inter-war period before large firms dominated the industry, many small engineers entered into motorcycle manufacture. One such was OEC at this small works. The high quality of their machines was reflected in their price and sales were too small. The advert is all that remains of the firm, but even this is now painted over. Photographed in 1975.

Portsmouth power station turbine room. The clean machinery and the white-coated operatives present a different image from that in many traditional activities. However, its costs were high and closure came in 1977. Photographed in 1972.

J.T. Sydenham timber yard, Mile End. Timber for housing in particular always ensured the need for timber importers who would normally have sawmills as part of their business. Typically their storehouses were open-sided and made of wood. That on the left has its roof carried on a Belfast truss. Photographed in 1973.

GULLETTING WHEEL
SPEED
1100 R.P.M

Above: J.T. Sydenham timber yard. The sawmill could hardly have been closer to the harbour, possibly facilitating imports. Photographed in 1972.

Left: J.T. Sydenham timber yard. The sawmill would cut timber into various shapes and sizes, the more intricate of which were achieved by a gulleting machine. Photographed in 1975.